The message we hear, as w͓
around us is that we are "en
could ever be enough to meet the difficulties and demands of
motherhood. That's why we need to hear the good news Christina Fox has packed into *Sufficient Hope*. We are not enough—
but Christ is sufficient! Each short chapter in this book is long on
good news—good news of grace to be thought through, chewed
on, and rested in.

> —**Nancy Guthrie**, Bible Teacher; Author, *The One Year Pray-
> ing through the Bible for Your Kids*

Motherhood often brings us to an end of ourselves. The sink
overflows with dishes, the longed-for naptime doesn't happen,
and the hearts of our children reveal fresh complexities every single day. Behind every trip to the playground and hand-print art
project is a woman who knows her own frailty. But, as Christina
Fox so helpfully reminds us, our weakness is simply an opportunity for us to cast ourselves on the One who is unfailingly strong.
With its practical examples, helpful prayers, and rich biblical
truth, *Sufficient Hope* is a gift to mothers. In these pages, both
new and experienced moms will find themselves reoriented away
from their own shortcomings and toward Christ's sufficiency.
Moms, take heart!

> —**Megan Hill**, Author, *Contentment: Seeing God's Goodness*;
> Editor, The Gospel Coalition

Sufficient Hope offers the life-giving refreshment of the gospel
for the real struggles and "not enoughness" of motherhood. Its
promises and prayers lift our eyes to behold Christ's sufficient
"enoughness" for this sacred calling of motherhood.

> —**Karen Hodge**, Coordinator of Women's Ministries, Pres-
> byterian Church in America; Coauthor, *Transformed: Life-
> taker to Life-giver* and *Life-giving Leadership*

I love the theological richness and practical wisdom in this book. As a grandmother, my first thought on reading it was, "I needed this book when our kids were young." Then I realized I still need this book now, to instruct and inspire me to live covenantally by praying for and encouraging young moms.

—**Susan Hunt**, Former Director of Women's Ministry, Presbyterian Church in America; Author, *Spiritual Mothering: The Titus 2 Model for Women Mentoring Women*

This is for the weary mom who needs a friend to point her to Jesus! Complete with guided prayers and thoughtful questions, this book provides accessible meditations that are full of lasting hope.

—**Emily Jensen**, Cofounder, Risen Motherhood

Motherhood is one of life's greatest blessings—and also one of life's greatest challenges. Many books for moms tell us what we need to do to succeed at motherhood. In contrast, Christina consistently points us to the hope we have in who Jesus is and what he has done for us. If you're exhausted from your efforts to be a better mom, come and find rest in Jesus.

—**Rachel Green Miller**, Author, *Beyond Authority and Submission: Women and Men in Marriage, Church, and Society*; Blogger, *A Daughter of the Reformation*

I have found that the greatest struggle I face in the Christian life is the struggle to find my joy in Christ rather than in the things of this world (such as my health, my accomplishments, my wife and children, my bank account, and so on). Mothers face this same struggle in unique ways, and that is why I am so excited about Christina Fox's new book, *Sufficient Hope*. With great humility, honesty, and humor, Christina looks at many of the struggles that mothers share in common and, in each case, points mothers to Christ as the only source of real and lasting joy. If you are a mother or would like to be a mother one day, you will want to read this book.

—**Guy Richard**, Executive Director and Assistant Professor of Systematic Theology, Reformed Theological Seminary, Atlanta

Motherhood doesn't afford much alone time, but it is so important to squeeze a few moments out of each day to refuel. Beautifully written, *Sufficient Hope* is just what the busy mom needs! Take a few minutes and fill your soul with these thoughtful and refreshing truths today!

—**Ruth Schwenk**, Founder, TheBetterMom.com; Author, *The Better Mom Devotional: Shaping Our Hearts as We Shape Our Homes*

Christina has become one of my favorite Christian authors. *Sufficient Hope* is full of encouragement for moms of all ages and in different seasons of parenting. This book offers us constant reminders to look to Christ, the Word of God, and the gospel throughout the joys and sometimes more difficult days of motherhood.

—**Coleen Sharp**, Co-host, *Theology Gals* Podcast

Christina Fox's *Sufficient Hope* appears at first glance to be wholly oriented to wives and mothers whose experiences have pushed them to the limit—and beyond. Yet husbands and fathers who sample this book will not only learn to empathize but also find that, just as for their wives, the promise that "I can do all things through Christ who strengthens me" (Phil. 4:13) points the way forward for them, too, as they face the demands of family life.

—**Kenneth J. Stewart**, Professor of Theological Studies, Covenant College, Lookout Mountain, Georgia

Do *you* have any thoughts on this book?
Consider writing a review online.
The author appreciates your feedback!

Or write to P&R at editorial@prpbooks.com with your
comments. We'd love to hear from you.

Sufficient Hope

Gospel Meditations and
Prayers for Moms

CHRISTINA FOX

P&R
PUBLISHING
P.O. BOX 817 • PHILLIPSBURG • NEW JERSEY 08865-0817

Unless otherwise indicated, Scripture quotations are from the ESV® Bible (The Holy Bible, English Standard Version®), copyright © 2001 by Crossway, a publishing ministry of Good News Publishers. Used by permission. All rights reserved.

Scripture quotations marked (NIV) are from the HOLY BIBLE, NEW INTERNATIONAL VERSION®. NIV®. Copyright © 1973, 1978, 1984 by International Bible Society. Used by permission of Zondervan Publishing House. All rights reserved.

Italics within Scripture quotations indicate emphasis added.

The opening quotes of chapters 1, 7, 8, 10, 11, and 15 are from Richard Rushing, ed., *Voices from the Past: Puritan Devotional Readings* (Edinburgh, UK: Banner of Truth Trust, 2009).

Portions of this book have been taken from the author's writings on her blog, www.christinafox.com, and revised and adapted for this format.

Printed in the United States of America

Library of Congress Cataloging-in-Publication Data

Names: Fox, Christina (Blogger), author.
Title: Sufficient hope : Gospel meditations and prayers for moms / Christina Fox.
Description: Phillipsburg, NJ : P&R Publishing Company, [2019]
Identifiers: LCCN 2019003258| ISBN 9781629954103 (pbk.) | ISBN 9781629954622 (epub) | ISBN 9781629954639 (mobi)
Subjects: LCSH: Mothers--Prayers and devotions. | Motherhood--Religious aspects--Christianity--Meditations. | Mothers--Religious life.
Classification: LCC BV4847 .F685 2019 | DDC 242/.6431--dc23
LC record available at https://lccn.loc.gov/2019003258

To my sister, Sabrina:

May Jesus be your all-sufficient hope
in every season of motherhood

Contents

Prayers

Acknowledgments

With each book I write, I become more aware of and grateful for the people and communities who help me in the process. From friends who pray to editors who read to readers who encourage, I am indebted to each and every person.

As always, I am thankful to my family: George, Ethan, and Ian. I could not write without their support and encouragement (and the time they leave me to do it!). I love you!

I am thankful to my agent, Don Gates, for his work on this project. Thanks, Don, for your encouragement, advice, and mentoring. A big thanks to Kristi James at P&R for her excitement and belief in the project. You are a joy to work with, and I am thankful to call you my friend. Thanks also to Amanda Martin, my editor. I appreciate your thoroughness, insight, and wisdom—all of which are essential to the writing process.

Just as C. S. Lewis needed the Inklings, writers need writing friends, and I am thankful to have writing friends who encourage and pray for me. Trillia Newbell, thanks for your generous encouragement. Megan Hill, it is a joy to pray with you regularly as we spur each other on in ministry. Rachel Miller, you are always an encouragement to me in my writing. I appreciate your wisdom and insight. Elizabeth Garn, Holly Mackle, and Liz Harper, thank you for your prayers and for checking in on my writing. To the enCourage team of writers, thank you for allowing me to be a part of your writing journey. As I read your words and edit them, I am shaped, exhorted, and encouraged in the faith. Thanks to my dear friends and constant cheerleaders: Lisa Tarplee, Cara Leger, and Marilyn Southwick. You have been there with me from the beginning. Thank you for your encouragement and prayers. Thanks to Karen Hodge for her friendship, mentorship, and encouragement. I love serving with you and your team at CDM. Thanks also to Debbie Locke, Amy Masters, Amy Nelson, Maryanne Helms, Jen Acklen, and Becky Jackson for their friendship, support, and encouragement. And to my Life Group—your prayers are appreciated!

To my readers, thank you for reading! You encourage me every day with your comments and messages. Many times, one of them comes just when I need it most—a gracious reminder that the Lord uses my jumbled, mixed-up, and sometimes even grammatically incorrect strings of words for his glory.

And above all, thanks to the Lord for the ever-humbling privilege to tell of his wonder through the written word! May he use the words in this book for his glory and fame.

Introduction

Have you ever wished you could take back something that you said in a particular moment? I've had plenty of such moments—but the one that stands out to me the most is a conversation I had with my midwife.

I went to see her after the birth of my first child. Like many first deliveries, mine was particularly complicated. I had numerous health problems afterward, and I arrived at the appointment hoping my midwife would help me to resolve them. I can still picture the room where I sat, with my son asleep in his carrier on the floor. I remember my midwife's kind eyes and gentle tone as she said, "I wonder if you might be suffering from postpartum depression."

Surprised, I dismissed the idea at once. I thought, *This is not depression. I know depression. I've diagnosed it and treated people for it. This is fatigue and stress from having a newborn and from being so sick.*

I shook my head. "I'm just exhausted. And stressed. I need to get my health problems under control. That's all." (There it is. That's the moment I wish I had said something like "You know, you might be right.")

Almost ten months later, I watched a show on television

in which a woman described her experience with postpartum depression. With tears streaming down my face, I whispered aloud, "That's me." I called my doctor the next day and got the help I needed.

When I had my second child, the postpartum depression returned. In many ways, I was prepared. I received medical care right away and implemented coping strategies that I knew would help. But I still struggled. Something was still missing. I couldn't quite put my finger on it, but I knew that I needed more. I arranged to meet with my pastor for counseling.

My pastor listened to me as I recounted everything I had done to make my life work: the coping skills I had used, the strategies I had implemented to improve my circumstances, and all the external solutions I had tried.

Then he looked me in the eyes and said, "But I haven't heard you tell me how you are trusting in what Christ already did for you."

I didn't say anything, because I was so confused. I had come to him looking for a way to make my life better—to make my life work. What he was giving me wasn't a solution.

He said it again. And then he went on to talk with me about what it means that Jesus lived a perfect life for me, died for me, and rose from the grave for me. He showed me how the gospel applied to my life as a mom—to my hard days, to my struggles to manage my life. This discussion was not based on some earth-shattering new concept. I already knew these things, but I had failed to live them out. My pastor reminded me that my hope and joy are found not in what I can do but in what Jesus has already done.

While I didn't leave my pastor's office that day cured and with all my problems solved, I did leave with a seed of hope. What he said to me about the gospel lingered. It burrowed into my heart and began to grow. As the months went on, I continued to return to that conversation in my mind, and hope continued to grow. Its roots dug deep and, over time, started to bear fruit. I began to look at all the circumstances and situations in my life through the lens of the gospel—through the truth of what Jesus had done for me.

And do you know what I learned? The gospel is sufficient. It is sufficient to give us help and hope.

Needless to say, I had a difficult start to motherhood. It did not begin the way I expected. Though there were certainly joys, an overall cloud followed me through those early years. Thankfully, the depression did go away, but the lessons I had learned from my pastor stayed with me. The truths of who Jesus is and what he came to do anchored me in my motherhood.

We each have our own challenges and difficulties in motherhood. You may have a child with a unique need. You may have your own health problems. Perhaps there are days when you just don't know what to do. You lack the wisdom that you need. Some days, you feel overwhelmed and don't have the strength to do what must be done. You feel stretched and pulled in multiple directions. You may have days when you feel weak and insufficient. And there are days when motherhood is downright hard.

No matter our stories or experiences, one thing is the same for all of us: *our need for Jesus.*

Hope for Moms

If you are reading this, I assume you are a mom. I'm a mom too. And, as moms, we often share our motherhood stories with one another. If we got together for a girls' night out or sat watching our kids play at a playdate, we'd likely exchange tales of hilarious things our children have said or done. You might share an embarrassing story of something that your child said (or yelled) while you were using a public restroom, and we'd share a laugh.

I might tell you about how I never corrected my youngest when he called lemonade "mellalade" because I thought it was so cute and how sad I was when he finally learned to say it correctly.

We'd also have stories to share of challenges we've faced as moms. Perhaps I'd tell you about the time one of my kids wandered off at the San Diego Zoo and how hard I cried when I finally found him. You might tell me about a chronic health problem that your daughter has and how desperate you are to learn its cause.

And then there are the hard and painful stories—the ones that break our hearts and keep us up at night. We might share concerns over our children's wandering hearts and temptations to sin or the special-needs issues one of our children battles with every day. Together, we'd lament each other's sorrows and fears.

Such stories vary from mom to mom, but we all have them. The truth is that, as moms, we will all experience both good times and hard times with our children. We will all laugh at our children's antics and smile over their unique idiosyncrasies. We will relish the joy of their hugs and kisses and enjoy reading them the same story at bedtime. Every. Single. Night.

Yet we will also weep over our children. We'll worry for our children. We will often be frustrated and probably even angry with our children. We'll face hardships with our children. Some of us may experience particularly hard times—such as disabilities or illnesses, behavioral challenges or limitations, relational barriers or conflicts.

Whatever experiences we face in motherhood, we all need Jesus—and he is sufficient. That's what this book is about: our need for the gospel of Jesus Christ. In every moment, in every season, and whatever our circumstances, the gospel is sufficient to give us hope.

Throughout this book, you'll find examples of challenges or difficulties that we all face in motherhood, such as fearing for our children, feeling weary and worn, being concerned over our children's sin, struggling with the identity issues we feel as moms, or wondering if our labors even matter. The gospel has something to say to these and to all the rest of our challenges.

The first two chapters lay the foundation for the book, and the following chapters look at specific aspects of motherhood through the lens of the gospel. Each chapter shows us our need for Jesus and his gospel. In addition, each chapter has a prayer to aid us in rehearsing the gospel, as well as a passage to read and reflect on.

Amazing growth happens in the context of community. Consider meeting together with other moms to read this book and learn from one another. The book can also be used in the context of discipleship relationships between older and younger women. No matter the season of motherhood we are in, we all need encouragement in the gospel.

It is my hope that this book would encourage you to turn to the truth of who Jesus is, and what he came to do, in every circumstance you face throughout motherhood. May you find your help and hope in him. And may your love for him grow as you consider all that he is for you.

Your sister in Christ,
Christina Fox

1

Jesus Is All-Sufficient

How blessed are we to enjoy this invaluable treasure, the love
of Christ; . . . Christ is our all, all other things are nothing.

Samuel Rutherford

Have you ever spent weeks, or maybe even months, planning for something . . . only to have it fall flat? Something unexpected cut into your perfectly laid plans, revealing just how little control you had over it all. You were left helpless and powerless. That happened to me during a recent holiday.

We rented a cabin in the mountains where our family could gather together and celebrate Thanksgiving. It was a beautiful stacked log cabin with a stone fireplace and a big front porch providing a clear view of mountains. The weather was cold and crisp, but also sunny and clear. Family drove in from hours away to celebrate with us.

In the weeks before the trip, I planned menus, carefully considering everyone's unique dietary needs and preferences. I thought through places to go and things that everyone, no matter their age or ability, could do. There were hikes I wanted to take, restaurants I wanted to try, and cute little gift shops I wanted to explore. Above all, I was excited to spend time with family who I don't often get to see.

Guess what happened? One person after another got sick—including me. I spent the final days of our trip in bed. And I completely missed one of the activities I had planned for us all to do. The holiday that I worked so hard to plan and prepare for will likely go down in the family history books as "the Thanksgiving when we all got so sick," rather than the trip I planned it to be.

We Need Jesus

It often takes an interruption like that for me to remember that I am not in control. That I don't have it all together. That I am dependent on another. This is a truth I have had to face countless times in motherhood, as well. In fact, if there's one thing that motherhood has taught me, it's that I can't do it on my own. I need help from outside myself. This is a humbling reality for me, as I have always been an independent sort. When I have a goal, I work hard and pursue it. I may seek advice or assistance along the way, but ultimately I know that if I want to get where I'm headed, I have to do the work that's required.

I faced motherhood the same way. I'm not a fly-by-the-seat-of-my-pants kind of person; I like to be prepared. So I bought all the books, studied all the methods, and read all the research. I applied myself to motherhood the same way that I did to a project or paper in college. I put everything into it the same way as I did my work. But unlike other things in my life, motherhood did not fit so neatly into a box. My children did not always conform to what the books said. The methods often failed. The research often turned out meaningless.

As a result, I was humbled. Like the stretch marks that are forever etched in my skin, motherhood stretched me farther than I was capable of stretching on my own. I learned that I was weak and insufficient and couldn't rely on my own resources or strength. I couldn't depend on my own wisdom. I couldn't find help and hope by studying methods. I couldn't make life work for me.

I needed Jesus. Of course, I had always needed Jesus; all of us need him in every stage of life. It's just that God often uses motherhood, with all its challenges and difficulties, to put that need front and center before us.

Motherhood reveals our need for a Savior. No matter the season our children are in—infancy and early childhood, adolescence, and beyond—we need Jesus to carry us through. We need Jesus to be our strength and wisdom. We need Jesus to redeem and rescue us from ourselves. We need Jesus to be our constant through the ups and downs of motherhood. In all the seasons of motherhood, the gospel becomes more beautiful to us in richer and deeper ways than ever before.

As we move through this book, I want to point you to Jesus, to your need for him, and to his sufficiency for you in your motherhood. No matter what your story is, no matter what circumstances you are going through, no matter what challenges your children face, Jesus is all-sufficient. You have hope in him, because of who he is and what he has done.

Our Preeminent Savior

It's fitting that we begin by focusing on Jesus and on who he is. In the book of Colossians, Paul described Jesus in near poetic terms. Some think that perhaps he used the words from an early hymn.

He is the image of the invisible God, the firstborn of all creation. For by him all things were created, in heaven and on earth, visible and invisible, whether thrones or dominions or rulers or authorities—all things were created through him and for him. And he is before all things, and in him all things hold together. And he is the head of the body, the church. He is the beginning, the firstborn from the dead, that in everything he might be pre-eminent. For in him all the fullness of God was pleased to dwell, and through him to reconcile to himself all things, whether on earth or in heaven, making peace by the blood of his cross. (Col. 1:15–20)

In my ESV Bible, the heading that precedes this passage reads "The Preeminence of Christ." The word *preeminence* is not one that we use every day (probably because there is little we could use it for!). *Preeminence* means superiority. It comes from the Greek word *proteuo*, which means to be first in rank or influence.[1] From it we get words like *protagonist*, the lead character in a story, or *prototype*, which is the first model of something.

Paul wrote that Christ is "the beginning, the firstborn from the dead, that in everything he might be preeminent." In describing Christ this way, he tells us something important. Christ is to be first and foremost in our lives. He is to have exalted status. He should be far and above everything else. He should be supreme in our thoughts, desires, loyalties, motivations, and actions.

In this passage, Paul tells us why: Christ is the second person of the Trinity—he is God. He existed before time began. Through him all things were created. Everything was created for him. He rules over all—both the seen and the unseen—including all those who rule in power. He also sustains all things; he keeps creation working and functioning as it should.

In the same way that he is first over creation, he is also first over the church. He created her. Through the blood that he shed on the

---

1. See James Strong, *The New Strong's Expanded Exhaustive Concordance of the Bible* (Nashville: Thomas Nelson, 2010), Strong's number 4409.

cross, he formed the church. He is her head, and she is his body. Because of his atoning work on the cross, we receive redemption from sin and peace with God. He reconciles us with God.

To sum up this passage, *Christ is Lord of all.*

This same Jesus—the one who flung the stars across the sky, the one whose hands were pierced for your sins—is the one who is sufficient for you in your motherhood. He carries, strengthens, and sustains you. He is your wisdom. He is your redemption. He is your peace.

As my pastor so helpfully reminded me when I struggled with depression, who Jesus is, and what he came to do, are sufficient to give us help and hope. Will you join me in praying the prayer on the following page?

For a Mom's Heart

1. Read 2 Corinthians 4. How is Christ exalted in Paul's life? How does Paul view his weaknesses? What is the "treasure in jars of clay"?
2. What would it look like for Jesus to be preeminent in your life as a mom?
3. Turn to God in prayer, exalting Jesus for who he is for you.

A Gospel Prayer on Christ's Sufficiency

. . . that in everything he might be preeminent. (Col. 1:18)

Dear Father in heaven,

I come before you, today, overwhelmed by life. The challenge of juggling motherhood and other responsibilities is often more than I can carry. As I read this passage about Christ's preeminence, I am reminded that while I am not sufficient in myself, he is sufficient for me. He rules over all things, from creation to the church—including my motherhood. I can trust him to be for me what I am not.

Forgive me for failing to exalt Jesus for who he is. Forgive me for thinking that I can do life apart from him. Forgive me for seeking strength and wisdom outside of him. Forgive me for not making Christ supreme in my life.

Help me to turn to Christ and keep him first and foremost in my life. May he have the preeminence in my thoughts, goals, and plans. May he be preeminent in my motherhood. May he be Lord of all.

Because of Jesus, and in his name, I pray. Amen.

2

The Good News Moms Need

Since He has gone up there, and is in heaven for us,
let us note that we need not fear to be in this world.

JOHN CALVIN

Consider the things that you did today. Did you wake up before everyone else and prepare for the day? Did you pack lunches for the kids or prepare homeschool lessons or send off some last-minute emails before work?

Perhaps you and your husband tag-teamed waking up the kids, getting them breakfast, and taking them to school. Perhaps you spent the day at work, in and out of meetings, while also trying to check in with the pediatrician about your little one's chronic ear infections. Or maybe you ran errands all morning, with one kid in the front of the cart and another in the back, and somehow managed to squeeze groceries in among all the moving body parts as well. Your to-do list may have also included paying some bills, tackling the pile of laundry, helping with homework, and driving a child or two to a playdate, sport, or other activity.

Did your day then end with the nightly ritual of bath time, stories, prayers, and hugs goodnight?

In all that you did throughout the day, and wherever you spent it, did you consider the gospel? Did you dwell on the truths of what Jesus did? Did those truths intersect with any of the activities, labors, conversations, or challenges you encountered in your day? Were you reminded of Christ's sufficiency for you? And, if so, did this shape your day and point you to your hope in Christ?

This book is about the gospel's sufficiency to give moms hope in their motherhood. In this chapter, I will talk about the gospel, what I mean by that word, and how it applies to all of life.

The Gospel of Jesus

We all know what it's like to try to communicate with someone who doesn't understand us. We may find ourselves repeating what we're trying to say or asking questions to figure out exactly what is causing the confusion. Often, the words that we use are part of the problem. Sometimes one person uses a word differently from the other. We may have a conversation that is centered on one topic, but if our definition of that topic differs, we will likely pass by each other in our attempts to understand.

Words are important—so let's take a look at the word *gospel*. I'll be using it a lot throughout this book, and I want to make sure its definition is clear. Our English word *gospel* comes from the definition of the Greek word *euangelion*.[1] This word is made up of the prefix *eu-*, which means "good" or "well," and the word *angelos*, which means "messenger."[2] The word *gospel* means "good message" or "good news."

1. See James Strong, *The New Strong's Expanded Exhaustive Concordance of the Bible* (Nashville: Thomas Nelson, 2010), Strong's number 2098.
2. Strong, Strong's number 32.

In the Old Testament, the term "good news" usually refers to just that: good news. It refers to someone announcing something good—as in the proverb "Like cold water to a thirsty soul, so is good news from a far country" (Prov. 25:25) and this passage from Isaiah: "How beautiful upon the mountains are the feet of him who brings good news, who publishes peace, who brings good news of happiness, who publishes salvation, who says to Zion, 'Your God reigns'" (Isa. 52:7).

In the New Testament, the word *gospel* or "good news" takes on a deeper and more specific meaning. It begins with an announcement of good news: a baby has been born. "Fear not, for behold, I bring you good news of great joy that will be for all the people. For unto you is born this day in the city of David a Savior, who is Christ the Lord" (Luke 2:10–11). A baby is certainly good news already; but the good news of the *gospel* is that this baby grew up to be a Savior—Christ the Lord.

After Jesus returned to heaven and the disciples began their ministry, the word *gospel* grew to refer to the good news of who Jesus is and what he came to do. The first four books of the New Testament came to be called "gospels" because they were about Jesus, his life, and what he did for us. The reformer John Calvin used the word *gospel* to refer to all that Jesus did: "how our Lord Jesus Christ came into the world, He went about, He died, He rose again, He ascended into heaven. That, I say, comes under the title 'Gospel.'"[3]

A number of years ago, the late David Nicholas filled the pulpit for a while at a church that our family attended in Florida. He used to say that you can't preach the good news without the bad news first; many of his sermons centered around what he called the "bad news / good news." It's true—we can't embrace or

---

3. John Calvin, *Sermons on the Deity of Christ* (Audubon, NJ: Old Paths Publications, 1997), 14.

appreciate the good news of the gospel without first understanding what makes it so good. That's where the bad news comes in.

The bad news is that we are sinners. We don't just commit sins—we are sinners. It is a nature we inherited from our first parents, Adam and Eve. When they first sinned by eating from the Tree of Knowledge of Good and Evil, sin entered the world. It seeped into all creation, including the heart of mankind.

Because God is holy and righteous, anything and anyone who is not holy and righteous cannot be in his presence. Even one sin is enough to keep us separated from God—and we sin countless times a day! As sinners, we deserve God's wrath and the punishment for sin: eternity in hell. God is judge of all the world, and that is his verdict. He established the sacrificial system in the Old Testament to show that blood had to be shed in order for sin to be forgiven. But animal sacrifices were not sufficient to reconcile people to God. The sacrifices had to be repeated over and over—day in and day out, year after year.

That's why the good news is so good. God the Father sent God the Son, Jesus Christ, to take on human flesh. He entered this sinful, broken world as a baby and lived a perfect life. He lived thirty-three years without sin and then became the perfect sacrifice, taking on our sins for us at the cross. He stepped in as a final substitute and took the punishment that we deserved. He suffered, died, and was buried. He then rose again from the grave three days later. Because he was righteous, the grave could not hold him. He ascended into heaven, where he stands at the right hand of God—ready and waiting to return once and for all to make things right and to bring us to be with him for eternity.

Through faith in Jesus Christ, we are saved from our sins. We are justified. This is a legal act, through which God declares us righteous and forgives us of all our sin. We are then adopted into God's family. Through our adoption, we become his children, fellow believers become our siblings, and Jesus becomes our elder brother. As children of God, we have all the rights and privileges that come with being his children and heirs of his kingdom.

And there's more! Faith unites us to Christ—we are one with him (see John 17:22–23). The apostle Paul called this being "in Christ." Through this union, all that he has done becomes ours. God looks at us and sees Jesus's righteousness. The death that he died is ours; his resurrection from the grave is ours. Through this union, we receive all the benefits of our salvation—our salvation is "in Christ," our sanctification is "in Christ," and our future glorification is "in Christ." We abide in Christ, and he abides in us. Through him, we bear fruit. Apart from union with Christ, we can do nothing (see John 15:5).

As you can see, the gospel is more than what happened in one moment at the cross. It's more than coming forward to an altar call. It is life-altering, sin-shattering, better-than-the-best-news-you've-ever-heard good news.

Yet this good news is only good news if it does something— if it impacts us in some way. When soldiers win a battle, news of their victory impacts the course of the war. When we embrace the good news, by faith, as a gift of God's grace (more good news!), the truths of the gospel transform our lives. We are no longer the same.

That's why it's so important for a word as common as *gospel* to be understood and made clear. Some people don't use it the way Scripture does. Some view the gospel as something you agree with before moving on with the rest of your life. Some view it as insurance that things will be okay after they die, and they don't give it a second thought after signing on the dotted line. Some see it as an opportunity for a redo in life—as though it wipes their slate clean and gives them a chance to get things right the second time. That's not the gospel. It's not a one-time thing. It's a truth that we turn to over and over throughout our lives—that we appropriate and apply to our hearts. The gospel is something that we never outgrow and never get beyond our need for.

The truths of who Jesus is and what he has done for us don't only save us for eternity (as major as that already is!); they also transform our daily lives in the here and now. They impact how we work, how we play, how we interact with others, how we face challenges, and how we suffer. They transform how we respond to our sin and to the sin of others. They give us hope when we are hopeless, peace when we are fearful, and joy when we are despairing. In fact, it will take an eternity to plumb the depths of the gospel's significance to our lives.

For a Mom's Heart

1. Read Ephesians 1. What gospel truths does Paul point to in the first half of the chapter? Look at his prayer for the Ephesians. What gospel truths does he pray for them?
2. Have you ever made considering the gospel part of your day-to-day routine? What impact did this have on your mind and heart?
3. Take time to pray today, thanking the Lord for the good news of the gospel.

A Gospel Prayer of Good News

... which now has been manifested through the appearing of our Savior Christ Jesus, who abolished death and brought life and immortality to light through the gospel. (2 Tim. 1:10)

Dear Father in heaven,

I hear good news all the time. I hear about an unexpected year-end bonus or about a friend's long-awaited pregnancy or that my favorite team won a game. Such news makes me excited. I want to throw a party and celebrate!

How much more should I rejoice in and celebrate the best news that ever was? The good news of the gospel outshines every other news. It's life-altering, life-transforming, life-sustaining good news. How much should the news of your Son, Jesus Christ, stand out above all other news!

Father, forgive me for not living like the gospel is the best news I've ever heard. Forgive me for living like it's old news. Forgive me for all the ways I have not allowed the good news of the gospel to shape my life.

I pray that as I take the time to consider the gospel and how it intersects and transforms my life, it would indeed become good news to my heart. That I would rejoice in it each day. That I would share it with those around me. That it would shape how I live. And that it would shape how I mother my children.

Thank you for the good news of Jesus Christ.

In his name I pray. Amen.

3

Remember the Good News

Every day [our Lord Jesus Christ] should be our
excellent mirror wherein we behold how much God
loves us and how well, in his infinite goodness, he has
cared for us in that he gave his dear Son for us.

MARTIN LUTHER

Since becoming a mom, I have found myself forgetting things.
I call it having "mommy brain." I've forgotten my kids' doctors'
appointments, remembering them only when I receive a call from
the doctor's office asking why we didn't show. I often walk into a
room and forget why I'm there. I put cereal boxes in the fridge
and return juice to the pantry. And I always call my kids by the
wrong name.

My boys ask me all the time to remind them to do something,
and I think, "Are you kidding me? I can't even remember what day
it is and what I'm supposed to be doing. How can I remind you
of anything?"

Over the years, I've developed habits to help myself remember things. Sometimes I leave a note on the bathroom mirror to

remind myself of an important meeting the next morning. I set reminders on my phone to alert me. And I regularly review my calendar. (I haven't figured out how to fix my cereal-box-in-the-fridge problem, though!)

Humans are prone to forgetfulness. Putting clothes in the dryer and forgetting to start it can be irritating. Doing an entire grocery-store run only to forget the one thing that we needed may even be funny. Neither is as detrimental as forgetting the good news of the gospel or as harmful as failing to live out the gospel in our lives. Mommy forgetfulness pales in comparison to gospel forgetfulness.

I guess that's why Scripture often talks about remembering or recalling what God has done. Israel was charged with celebrating regular feasts and holidays so that they would recall what God had done for them in the past. Our Savior implemented a special meal, the Lord's Supper, as a special time for us to remember what he did for us in the gospel. And every time the early church struggled or wandered in their faith or faced hardship, the New Testament writers pointed them to the truths of who Jesus is and what he has done.

Remembering the Gospel

As moms whose hearts are prone to forgetfulness, we need to remind ourselves of the gospel on a regular basis. We need to remember the good news until it saturates our hearts and becomes our personal anthem. Some people call this "preaching the gospel to yourself." This simply means reviewing, and reminding ourselves, who Jesus is and what he came to do.

When we battle sin in our lives, we remind ourselves that we have a great Savior who lived the life that we could not live. We rejoice over his perfect record that was credited to us. We remember the death that he died to pay for our sin. We pray, repent of our sins, and ask God to forgive us because of Jesus's sacrifice for us. We take great hope in the fact that, because he ascended into heaven, he now stands before the Father interceding for us.

When we face hardship or trials in our lives, we remember our Savior, who left the riches of heaven in order to live in this fallen world. We remember that he grew up in poverty, as the son of a carpenter—that he knew what it is to be hungry and homeless, for he never had a home of his own. We remember the loss and grief that he felt when his friend Lazarus died and the rejection and abandonment that he experienced when he needed his disciples most and they deserted him. We remember how he never gave in to Satan's offerings during his temptation in the wilderness. Most of all, we remember the suffering that he faced for us at the cross. Because he conquered death and rose from the grave, we know that our sufferings will have an end. One day we will shed our sin for good and join him in eternity.

When life is busy and hectic and overwhelming, we remember our Savior. Because we are united to him by faith, he is our strength in all things. He sustains us with his Word. He gives us grace to endure. He is our peace in the chaos. Because he went to great lengths to rescue us and redeem us from sin, we know he is with us in whatever we encounter or struggle with throughout our day.

In all these ways and more, we remember who Christ is and what he has done. Whatever is happening in our lives as moms— whether we are wrangling our kids into the car, washing dishes, paying bills, or heading to work—the gospel is applicable. It matters to our lives. In both the big and the small things, it shapes who we are.

Ways to Remind Yourself of the Gospel

What are some practical ways we can reinforce the truths of the gospel?

Read and Study Scripture

Primarily, it's the Bible that teaches us about the gospel. The Old Testament shows us our need for a Savior, and the New Testament tells us who he is and what he did for us. The gospels are a biography of Jesus's life; they chronicle his teaching, healing, and preaching. The New Testament epistles unpack the gospel, its meaning, and its significance to our lives. Reading and studying God's Word helps us to grow in our understanding of the gospel, and our love for our Savior will grow as a result.

Set Your Mind on the Gospel

Throughout our day, we can set our mind on the truths of the gospel. We do this by countering sinful or wayward thoughts with the truth of who Jesus is and what he has done. We speak back to our thoughts with what we've learned in God's Word. When we find ourselves overwhelmed, worried, angry, and so on, we ask ourselves, "What does the gospel say to this?" When the storms of life rain down on us, we look to Christ—our anchor and hope. When we are tempted to sin, we exhort ourselves by reciting the truth of the gospel.

Read Books That Point to the Gospel

Many godly writers point us to Christ. Whether it is a book on theology, a devotional, or a Christian-living book, any book that is rooted in the gospel will encourage and exhort us to live out the gospel in our lives. No book is a substitute for reading Scripture, but books can be of help as supplements.

Listen to Worship Songs That Sing of the Gospel

We all know the power that music has to calm our hearts. When we listen to music that reminds us of the gospel, we can't help but worship our Savior. This is particularly helpful when we are overwhelmed by our emotions. Music can reach areas of our hearts that are hard to get to otherwise, and when music lifts high the name of Jesus and praises him for what he has done for us, we are drawn into his presence with thankful hearts.

Pray through the Gospel

While moms may find it challenging to set aside a significant block of time to read their Bibles each day, they can always pray. Prayer is something we can do while emptying the dishwasher, feeding the baby, or driving the car (as long as we do it with our eyes wide open!). And as we pray, we can pray through the gospel.

What does this look like? There's no formula for it, but whatever we are praying about, we can include the gospel in our prayers by praying through what Jesus has done. We can reinforce the gospel for ourselves in our prayers.

After all, we come to our Father in prayer because of what Christ has done. Through his perfect life and sacrificial death, the barrier that stood between us and God has been torn. The literal curtain in the temple stood as a stark reminder of our separation from God. But once Christ's sacrifice was complete, this curtain was torn and the barrier was removed. As Calvin noted,

> It [was not] proper that the veil should be rent, until the sacrifice of expiation had been completed; for then Christ, the true and everlasting Priest, having abolished the figures of the law, opened up for us by his blood the way to the heavenly sanctuary, that we may no longer stand at a distance within the porch, but may freely advance into the presence of God. . . . Thus the rending of the veil was not only an abrogation of the ceremonies which existed under the law, but was, in some respects, an opening of heaven, that God may now invite the members of his Son to approach him with familiarity.[1]

1. John Calvin, commentary on Matthew 27:51, trans. William Pringle,

This is why Paul wrote to the Ephesians, "In him and through faith in him we may approach God with freedom and confidence" (Eph. 3:12 NIV).

What a privilege it is to come before the throne of God and lay our prayers at his feet! How amazing it is that he hears our prayers! And not only that, but he desires for us to come to him. Prayer is how we communicate with God. It's also how he works in our lives. He uses our prayers to carry out his will, to draw us deeper into his grace, to reshape our thoughts and emotions, and to give us more of himself.

Dear friend, draw near to God. Cry out to him. As you do so, remember all that he has done for you in Christ.

For a Mom's Heart

1. Read Romans 6. How does the gospel transform our lives?
2. Do you remind yourself of the gospel (preach the gospel to yourself)? How can you do so today?
3. Turn to God in prayer and pray through the truths of the gospel, rejoicing in what Christ has done for you.

---

available online at "Calvin's Commentaries: Matthew 27," Bible Hub, accessed September 5, 2018, https://biblehub.com/commentaries/calvin/matthew/27.htm.

A Gospel Prayer to Remember Our Savior

If then you have been raised with Christ, seek the things that are above, where Christ is, seated at the right hand of God. Set your minds on things that are above, not on things that are on earth. For you have died, and your life is hidden with Christ in God. When Christ who is your life appears, then you also will appear with him in glory. (Col. 3:1–4)

Dear Father in heaven,

What a privilege and joy it is to come before you as your child. What amazing grace that you would give me the gift of faith and save me from my sins through the life, death, resurrection, and ascension of your Son. Thank you, Jesus, for this precious gift!

I pray that I would remember and rehearse all that Jesus has done, every day of my life. When I sin, help me to appropriate the gospel by turning to the cross in repentance and receiving your forgiveness. When I am tempted, help me to remember Jesus and the perfect life that he lived for me. When I'm afraid, help me to remember that, at the cross, Jesus conquered my greatest fear—separation from you. When I'm in despair, help me to remember that because Jesus conquered sin and death, one day he will return and wipe away all my tears. When I am weak, help me to remember that I am united to Christ by faith in the gospel and can therefore draw from his strength. Day after day, moment by moment, may I remember the gospel and apply it to all of my life.

You are always sufficient for me, Jesus.

Because of him I pray. Amen.

4

What Did You Expect?

If you have Christ, you have all. Do not be desponding,
do not give ear to the whisperings of Satan.

CHARLES SPURGEON

When you first learned that you were going to be a mom—
whether through a pregnancy test or a notification from an adoption agency—what did you imagine? What images came to your
mind? Did you picture cuddling up with your child on the couch
reading stories? Perhaps you imagined fun and laughter as you
blew bubbles together in the yard. Or maybe sweet smiles and
splashes at bath time.

Did you wonder what your child would be like? Did you
imagine your child as quiet and studious, as athletically gifted,
as friendly and outgoing? Did you picture what she or he would
look like, act like, and be like?

And what about yourself—how did you imagine yourself as
a mother? Did you picture yourself baking cookies and preparing
fun crafts to do each day? Did you see yourself as warm, kind,
and patient? Perhaps you imagined yourself as the fun mom—
always coming up with new and creative ideas and adventures. Or
as the wise mom who could answer any question. You may have

dreamed of all the things you would teach your child and of the experiences you would provide for your son or daughter.

Did you consider the challenges or hardships you would encounter as a mom? You may have been prepared for sleepless nights. You likely heard stories from friends about challenges with toddlers. Maybe you witnessed your nephew's or niece's tantrums at the dinner table. But overall, before we become moms, it's hard to imagine the difficulties we may face. And even if we could, there's no way for us to know what a particular difficulty will feel like or how it will impact us and our family.

Yet, no doubt, you have now experienced some level of difficulty—such as

- a chronically sick child
- a child with a disability
- a child with learning struggles
- a child whose temperament is the opposite of yours (or is too much the same)
- a child who struggles to make friends
- a child who is strong-willed

Or maybe the challenge has been within yourself, such as

- a battle with postpartum depression or anxiety
- a lack of patience
- boredom and/or dissatisfaction as a mom
- loneliness or isolation
- parenting responsibilities that fall to you on your own
- feelings of being overwhelmed
- your own health problems
- financial stressors that make it hard to provide what your child needs
- struggles to balance work and home life

In all these ways and more, the expectations that we have before we first hold our child in our arms clash head-on with the reality of what motherhood is like day in and day out.

You know those sweet baby shampoo commercials that show moms and babies bonding over bath time? Sometimes those commercials bring me to tears. Other times I want to yell, "Motherhood isn't always like that!"

Our expectations make a big difference in how we respond to things. Imagine receiving a birthday gift. You expect your husband to buy you a certain gift—after all, you did make a list that included links to the stores where he could purchase what you wanted. When you open your present, it's not what you expected. Not even close. He went completely off-list and got you something that you never wanted at all.

When we receive a different gift from the one we expected, our initial excitement quickly deflates. We feel disappointed and let down. We may wonder, "Why would he even think that I wanted that?"

When it comes to your expectations of motherhood, you may respond in multiple ways. You might respond in anger or frustration. You might think, "That's not fair!" You might look for someone or something to blame. You might even blame yourself. That anger, over time, grows into bitterness that seeps into everything you do.

You might respond with despair. The heavy weight of your circumstances bears down hard and keeps you from moving forward. You may want to give up. The life you once thought you would have is over—so why bother?

Or you might grow cynical, always expecting the worst. You might give up on hope and think there is no joy to be found in motherhood at all. This cynicism overshadows your motherhood, and everyone feels it—your children most of all.

It's important that we take an honest look at our expectations of motherhood. It's important that we acknowledge them and realize the impact they have on us. We need to measure our expectations with the truth. Because sometimes our expectations are simply wrong. Sometimes they are founded on truth but are exaggerated. Oftentimes, our expectations fail to account for the fall and its effect on our life. And above all, our expectations minimize the power of the gospel in our lives.

It's essential, then, that we know what the Bible tells us to expect from life.

The Story of Scripture

Scripture explains how we got where we are today. It explains why things don't work the way they should, what God did to fix it all, and what will happen at the end. Scripture's story of creation, fall, redemption, and restoration helps us understand the challenges that we face as moms. It helps us to see why our expectations fail and why life often seems unfair. It answers the question that we moms so often ask in our hearts: *Why?* As we remember this story, our eyes are opened and we are able to face our failed expectations—those things that we didn't see coming.[1]

This grand story starts with the story of creation. It tells us that God created the world. In the beginning, his world was a place of perfect harmony and peace. Everything worked as it should. Our first parents, Adam and Eve, lived in right relationship with their Maker and with each other. They knew God and were fully known by him. They found joy in each other and in their work together. They communicated without conflict. They were united and had no barriers between each other.

---

1. This section is inspired by a piece I wrote for *The Christward Collective*: see Christina Fox, "The Story and the Suffering," *The Christward Collective*, Alliance of Confessing Evangelicals, July 5, 2018, https://www.placefortruth .org/blog/the-story-and-the-suffering#.W4WF4OhKg2w.

This story tells us that the ache and longing that we feel for wholeness and healing are because things today are not as they were created to be. We all have the feeling that something is missing. Deep in our bones, we know that this world is not as it should be. The reason we expect life to work a certain way is because we know it's the way that things used to be. Deep down, we expect healthy children because God originally created us healthy. The reason we expect joy-filled motherhood is because that expectation is imprinted in the fiber of our being. The story of creation explains these longings.

The perfect world that God created was ruined when Adam and Eve listened to and believed Satan's lies. They desired to be like God and ate fruit from the tree he had instructed them not to eat. Their eyes were opened, and sin entered the world. They felt shame and covered themselves—and we have done the same ever since. We've inherited our first parents' sin nature, and we spend our lives hiding from God and attempting to cover the evidence of our sins. When our hearts cry out, "Why is life so hard? Why is motherhood not as I expected? Why is my child not what I expected?" we recall the story of the fall and remember that sin is the cause of all the brokenness and sorrow that we feel in this life—our own sin, the sin of others against us, and the effects of sin on the created world, which produce disease and the breakdown of all things. If our child has a disability or struggles in learning, this story explains why. Our child's sin and our own sinful responses to it can be traced back to the fall as well. The story of the fall also explains the playground bully who picks on our child.

After they sinned, God gave Adam and Eve the consequences that were due for their sin, and they were expelled from the garden. But before they left, God promised a Rescuer, a Redeemer, who would come and make all things right again (see Gen. 3:15). The rest of the Old Testament tells the story of the spread of sin. It shows the depths of our depravity and our need for salvation. It also reveals how God pushed forward his plan to fulfill his promise to redeem mankind.

When we want to know what God is doing about the sin and suffering in our world, we turn our aching hearts to the story of redemption. At just the perfect time in history, God stepped into our world. He covered himself with human flesh and lived the life that we could not live. Jesus Christ, the only Son of God, faced temptation, sorrow, rejection, pain, and suffering—but never sinned. Through his life, he showed the world who God is. He taught and healed and loved. He opened people's eyes to see what they needed most. He bore the curse for sin at the cross. Through faith in him, we are forgiven of our sins by his blood that was shed for us and are brought into the family of God. He rose victoriously from the grave, conquering death once and for all and ensuring that, one day, we too would rise to life eternal.

This is the story we need to remember and reflect on in our hearts. As we do so, we remember that Jesus is the Man of Sorrows who is familiar with grief. He knows what it is to face loss, abandonment, poverty, sickness, and temptation. We remember that his grace is sufficient to bear all our burdens, cares, sorrows, and sin. We remember that we have not only eternal hope but also present hope because of what Jesus did for us in his perfect life and sacrificial death. We remember that our personal heartaches, trials, and sufferings unite us to our suffering Savior and make us more like him. We find rest in the truth that because God went to great lengths to rescue us and redeem us from sin, he will certainly keep and preserve us during whatever we are currently going through. We find hope in the promise that Jesus is making all things new (see Rev. 21:5)—including our and our children's hearts.

Indeed, we will face failed expectations at some point in motherhood—but motherhood is a mixture of challenges as well as great joys, sweet moments, and fun memories. There's nothing else like watching our children grow and mature as they take their first steps, say their first words, and delight in the wonders of God's creation. Enjoying snuggles and story times and laughing at their silly antics is a blessing to treasure. It's a great gift to see God at work in our children's hearts and to help to disciple them in the faith. These joys are graces from God, and they remind us of the greater joy to come, in eternity, when we will be transformed and will reign with Christ forever.

Whatever we face in our day—whether hardship or joy—the grand story of the Bible gives shape to our expectations. It explains our longings. It gives hope to our struggles. And it points us to the glory to come.

Hope in Christ

The big story of Scripture centers on Christ, our Redeemer. When failed expectations hit hard and motherhood overwhelms us, we need to find hope in who Christ is for us.

Remember the following truths about Christ. Recite them aloud. Pray through them. Write them down and post them in places where you will see them. Rejoice over them. Share them with others.

- *He became sin for us.* "For our sake he made him to be sin who knew no sin, so that in him we might become the righteousness of God" (2 Cor. 5:21).
- *He bore our sins for us.* "He himself bore our sins in his body on the tree, that we might die to sin and live to righteousness. By his wounds you have been healed" (1 Peter 2:24).
- *He is our righteousness.* "And because of him you are in Christ Jesus, who became to us wisdom from God, righteousness and sanctification and redemption" (1 Cor. 1:30).

- *He intercedes for us.* "Who is to condemn? Christ Jesus is the one who died—more than that, who was raised—who is at the right hand of God, who indeed is interceding for us" (Rom. 8:34).
- *He strengthens and sustains us with himself.* "I am the bread of life; whoever comes to me shall not hunger, and whoever believes in me shall never thirst" (John 6:35).
- *He prepares us for eternity.* "Now may the God of peace himself sanctify you completely, and may your whole spirit and soul and body be kept blameless at the coming of our Lord Jesus Christ" (1 Thess. 5:23).

Dear friend, your life with your children will have joy, but it will also have sorrows. Often, motherhood won't fit what you imagined. Your children will struggle; you will struggle. Yet, while you may have big burdens and great cares, you have an even greater Savior. Turn to Jesus and keep your eyes fixed on him. Remember the story of redemption, and recite what God has done for you. Remember why things in life don't work out as they should, what God did about it through his Son, and how he gives you great hope for the future, when all things that are broken will be made whole.

While many of your expectations may fail, you can always expect great things from God.

For a Mom's Heart

1. Read Romans 8:18–39. What can you expect from God?
2. Do you ever struggle with failed expectations in your motherhood? How do you respond to them? What does the gospel have to say to you when this happens?
3. Turn to God in prayer. Repent of your responses to your failed expectations. Look to Christ and to who he is for you.

A Gospel Prayer for Failed Expectations

Now to him who is able to strengthen you according to my gospel and the preaching of Jesus Christ, according to the revelation of the mystery that was kept secret for long ages but has now been disclosed and through the prophetic writings has been made known to all nations, according to the command of the eternal God, to bring about the obedience of faith—to the only wise God be glory forevermore through Jesus Christ! Amen. (Rom. 16:25–27)

Dear Father in heaven,

I come before you overwhelmed. Frustrated. Sad, even. Motherhood has not been what I thought it would be. Oh, there are many joys: I cherish the sweet smiles and hugs from my children. I love when they giggle. I love seeing the light go on when they learn something new. And I dearly love my children. But at the same time, I feel angry and bitter over the struggles they have. To be honest, I don't think it's fair the things they have had to deal with in their lives. I also grieve my own struggles and the ways in which I have not been the mom I thought I would be.

What I need is a fresh reminder of who you are and what you have done. I picked up my Bible for encouragement, and instead of zeroing in on a specific verse, I remembered the big story you tell: the meta-story of Scripture. As I thought about how you created all things and how perfect everything was in the garden, it made me realize why I have this unmet longing for things to be different than they are. I remembered what happened when Adam and Eve sinned and how it impacted all of creation—right down to my very own heart today. The spread of sin has seeped into every crack and crevice of this world. I was reminded why my children suffer and why I suffer and why motherhood hasn't been all it's cracked up to be. But then I remembered the good news: you sent your Son to redeem us from sin. I thank you for your grace for me in Christ. I thank you for the hope of eternity and for the good news that will come at the end of the story, when what is broken will be made whole once and for all.

Forgive me, Father, when my expectations for my life are wrong. Forgive me for not comparing those expectations with your Word. Forgive me for my sinful responses to those expectations. Help me not to harbor bitterness or to give up on joy in motherhood. Help me not to be cynical or to always expect the worst in life. Help me instead to hope in Christ.

Thank you, Jesus, for all that you are for me. Thank you that, even though life is not as I expected, you are with me in it. Help me to keep my eyes fixed on you.

May my expectations always be shaped by your Word.

In Jesus's name, amen.

5

Helpless but Never Hopeless

May we be in You as a branch is in the stem, and may we
bear fruit from You. Without You we can do nothing.

C. H. SPURGEON

The day my first child was born, our community had just endured a Category 3 hurricane. Power was out everywhere. The hospital was damaged, which meant that people recovering from surgery were in the maternity ward along with all the women—including myself—who had gone into labor as a result of the storm. I had complications after the birth and had to stay a few days longer. Everything was chaos around me as exhausted doctors and nurses worked overtime. I wasn't allowed to sit up in bed and had to lie still for three days, which made it hard to handle a newborn.

The feeling of helplessness that was birthed in that hospital room followed me home, never to leave my side.

I don't know about you, but I don't like feeling helpless. I like knowing what to do in every circumstance. I like to be equipped, prepared, and ready. I like to have plans in place in order to prevent chaos. I like to control the unexpected. But, as I quickly learned, there's no controlling motherhood.

My feelings of helplessness continued as my oldest and, later, my youngest battled asthma and chronic infections. They were sick for most of their early childhood, which meant middle-of-the-night breathing treatments and visits to specialists. Eventually, they both ended up having sinus surgery. And in each moment of their sickness, I felt helpless.

When I find myself repeating the same rule or the same instruction I have repeated each day for years and no one seems to catch on and learn from it, I feel helpless. When my children are struggling with friends or a difficult teacher, or are experiencing the natural consequences of their choices, I feel helpless. Today, as I navigate the struggles and challenges of their middle and high school years, I continue to feel helpless. Every day is a journey into the unknown.

But the truth is that, while I may often feel helpless as a mom, I am never hopeless. Never. And neither are you.[1]

Helpless but Never Hopeless

While feeling helpless is something that I resist, it's exactly what Christ has called me to be. He didn't come for those who have it all together, who know everything, and who don't need any help. He came to rescue and redeem those who are just like me—the helpless.

For the Son of Man came to seek and to save the lost. (Luke 19:10)

1. This chapter is inspired by a post I wrote for Risen Motherhood: see Christina Fox, "For the Mom Who Feels Helpless," Risen Motherhood, February 22, 2018, https://www.risenmotherhood.com/blog/for-the-mom-who -feels-helpless.

Those who are well have no need of a physician, but those who are sick. I came not to call the righteous, but sinners. (Mark 2:17)

Isn't that a marvelous truth? God doesn't expect us to have it all together. He doesn't expect us to know what to do in every situation and to ooze mommy strength and confidence. He came to be hope for the helpless. If you are feeling helpless today, you are exactly where you need to be.

Jesus Christ came to rescue you and me from our greatest problem: the sin that separates us from God. He came to live the life that we could not live and to die the death that we deserved for our sin. In doing so, he rescued us from our slavery to sin. He freed us from trying to live life on our own apart from God. He delivered us from seeking our hope outside of him. And he has promised to be for us what we can't be for ourselves. This is the truth we must cling to: when we are weak, he is strong.

As wisdom incarnate, Christ knows just what to do all the time and in every circumstance (see Col. 2:3). He is never helpless, lost, or confused. He is never overwhelmed by the storms and challenges of life. He's never weak or insufficient. He's never surprised by anything. He reigns over all things—including our seemingly hopeless circumstances. For those of us who are helpless, with Christ is exactly where we need to be.

In Mark 4, the disciples were out on the Sea of Galilee when a storm arose. As seasoned fishermen, they were used to storms on the water. But this one was so strong and fierce that they thought they would die.

And a great windstorm arose, and the waves were breaking into the boat, so that the boat was already filling. But he was in the stern, asleep on the cushion. And they woke him and said to him, "Teacher, do you not care that we are perishing?" And he awoke and rebuked the wind and said to the sea, "Peace! Be still!" And the wind ceased, and there was a great calm. He said to them, "Why are you so afraid? Have you still no faith?" And they were filled with great fear and said to one another, "Who then is this, that even the wind and the sea obey him?" (vv. 37–41).

They had done all that they knew to do in the midst of a ferocious squall, but it wasn't enough. While they tried to fend for themselves, Jesus, exhausted from a long day of teaching, slept in the stern of the boat. I can almost hear the panic in the disciples' voices as they cried out, "Don't you care?" But Jesus, the Maker and Ruler of the wind and the waves, had only to say, "Be still!" and all was calm. The calm didn't come on gradually, the way the seas slowly stop their seizing once a storm has passed. Rather, just like that first day when God spoke the world into being, this storm came to an instant stop at the sound of its Maker's voice.

The disciples immediately switched from fearing the storm to fearing the Lord. "And they were filled with great fear and said to one another, 'Who then is this, that even the wind and the sea obey him?'" (v. 41).

The disciples were helpless—but they had never been hopeless. The very God who rules over all creation, including the wind and the waves, was with them in the storm. Though they felt helpless, though they didn't know what to do, Christ was with them. He was their hope and help.

Christ Is Our Hope

Too often, I forget that I'm not hopeless. I try to mother my children in my own strength and wisdom. I research and Google and pin and read everything I can get my hands on, and I still feel inadequate to the task of motherhood. Problems arise, and I get overwhelmed. I worry and despair. I feel like a failure. I fret and fear that motherhood will sink me.

As we saw in chapter 3, we often forget the hope that we have in Christ. When I strive in my motherhood apart from Christ, I've forgotten who he is and what he has done. When I try to control my life and the chaos of parenting, when I put my trust in systems and methods and lists to make my life work, and when I fret and worry that motherhood is too big and I'm too weak, I've forgotten my source of life and hope.

In all our helpless situations, Christ is our hope. He has redeemed us from our sin and given us his righteousness. Through our faith in his perfect life, sacrificial death, and glorious resurrection, we are made right with God. And as Paul reminds us, if God has given his own Son to rescue us from sin, how can he not also give us all things (see Rom. 8:32)? If God has given us Christ, how can we think he won't meet us in our daily struggles and challenges? How can we think he would leave us to drown in motherhood? By providing for us when we were at our most helpless—when we were trapped in sin and separated from God—Christ proved that he is our hope.

The disciples cried out, "Don't you care?" Have you ever felt like crying that out, yourself? On those really hard days when the kids are doing the opposite of everything you say, when your husband is out of town and you are on your own, when you are exhausted and spent, do you ever wonder whether God even cares? Christ's sacrifice for us on the cross is his response: a resounding yes! When we were at our most helpless, and when we continue to feel helpless in smaller ways every day, Christ is our hope. He rules over all things. He knows all things. He bears all our burdens and hears our every cry. He works all our circumstances together for our ultimate good. He is our comfort, our peace, and our rest.

When the storms of life crash over us, we must turn to Christ.

When we don't know what to do in our mothering, we must turn to Christ. When we are overwhelmed and weak and don't know which way to go, we must turn to Christ. We must cry out to him. We must remember what he has done for us in his perfect life and sacrificial death. We must rely on his strength, wisdom, power, and truth—not on our own. We must find our peace and solace in him. We must remember that he rules over the details of motherhood.

Yes, we may often find ourselves feeling helpless; but in Christ we have everything we need, for he is right there in the storm with us—ruling and reigning and being for us what we can't be for ourselves.

Dear friend, you may often feel helpless as a mom. But in Christ you are never hopeless.

For a Mom's Heart

1. Read Philippians 3:1–11. John Calvin refers to "confidence in the flesh" as "everything that is apart from Christ."[2] In what ways have you sought confidence in your flesh? What did Paul think of his achievements, and in what did he place his confidence?

2. How are you feeling hopeless today? What gospel truths can you cling to?

3. Pray to the Lord, and seek his help and hope.

[handwritten notes: mean wife / bad mom / feed my kids too much sugar / bad friend / old for you / you are redeemed / you are loved / you are known by christ]

2. John Calvin, commentary on Philippians 3:3, trans. John Pringle, available online at "Calvin's Commentaries: Philippians 3," Bible Hub, accessed May 11, 2018, http://biblehub.com/commentaries/calvin/philippians/3.htm.

[handwritten notes: Jesus is for you / What you can't be / for yourself]

A Gospel Prayer for the Helpless

For we are the circumcision, who worship by the Spirit of God and glory in Christ Jesus and put no confidence in the flesh. (Phil. 3:3)

Dear Father in heaven,

I come before you today feeling helpless. Insufficient. Overwhelmed. Motherhood is harder than I ever thought it would be. Just when I think I know what to expect, the kids move into a new stage. I don't know how to face these challenges. I don't know how to be the mom they need me to be.

It's so hard to juggle all the details of parenting. I have to be on top of all their needs: physical, social, spiritual, emotional, developmental, academic, and more. And much of it I am simply not prepared for. I simply don't know the answers. Every morning when I wake up, it feels like it's final exam week and I'm not ready. What if I fail? What if I let my kids down?

Forgive me for putting confidence in my flesh. Forgive me for striving to do motherhood in my own strength. Forgive me for not turning to you for hope and help and for seeking life outside you. Forgive me for seeking hope in things and circumstances. Forgive me for trying to control everything.

My flesh will fail me, but Christ never will. Instead of putting my confidence in the flesh, I am to find my hope in what Christ has done. Jesus came to do what I could not do. He came to live the life I could not live. I thank you that, because of Jesus, when you look at me you don't see my failures as a mom. You don't see how insufficient I am. You see the sufficiency of Jesus and the perfect life that he lived for me.

You know the storms of my life. You know how hard these days have been. You know just what I need—even before I do. Please be my strength. Please help me to look to you as my hope when I feel helpless. Help me not to get caught up in what's happening in my life, and with my children, but to seek you as my sufficiency.

Give me grace in every moment to glorify you in the decisions I make, in the way I respond to my children, and in the way I navigate unfamiliar territory with them.

In Jesus's name, amen.

6

The Work That's
Never Done

*Faith in Him who gave Himself for us leads us to spend
our energies in His service and to do our ordinary work
with an eye to His Glory—and so our life is colored
and savored by our faith in the Son of God.*

CHARLES SPURGEON

Years ago, I spent months working on a book proposal. Various
friends then spent weeks helping me to edit it. And then it was
rejected by more publishers than I care to recount. Since then, it
has remained tucked away in the depths of my computer files—
and, if it were possible, collecting dust.

One of the hardest things about writing is when something
that you write isn't used. When I spend hours crafting just the
right sentence, when I've woven my heart and soul into each
paragraph of a work, and it is never read, it makes all the time,
effort, and energy seem like a waste. It's disheartening and dis-
couraging.

But writing isn't the only thing I put energy into that no one sees. Countless things that I work on throughout the day go unnoticed by those around me. The laundry that I fold and put away. The items that I pick up off the floor and return to their rightful places. The time and effort that I pour into my children's hearts and spiritual growth. My intercessory prayers for God to be at work in them. Decisions and choices that I make for the benefit of those around me. The time and effort that I sacrifice in order to serve and provide. When I don't see the fruit of that work, sometimes I grow weary and wonder, *Is it worth it?*

Motherhood is filled with repetitive duties: changing diapers, making lunches, teaching and reteaching our children the same lessons. Not to mention taking our kids to the pediatrician, making sure they have clothes and shoes that fit for their first day back at school, and keeping track of who needs to go where and when. It's hard to clean up a mess of toys and know that we'll just have to do it again in a few hours. It's often disheartening to know that the discussions we have with our children about kindness and sharing with others will have to be reviewed again and again before they sink in. Sometimes we get to the end of a day and feel like nothing of significance has been accomplished. We've worked hard—but what do we have to show for it? As a result, we can feel discouraged. We may wonder whether our families realize all that we do for them and if they take our efforts for granted.

If our families don't notice and express thanks for what we do, they should. Gratitude is the proper response to someone working on our behalf. But whether or not our families notice, we can remember this truth: God sees our labors on behalf of our children and family. He never misses our efforts or takes them for granted. He knows all the mundane tasks and repeated duties we have performed. And when we labor for him, he is glorified.

All Work Is for His Glory

We were created for a purpose: to glorify God and enjoy him forever, as the Westminster Catechisms tell us.[1] This is what we are called to do, in all things big and small—in the important and the seemingly unimportant.

> So, whether you eat or drink, or whatever you do, do all to the glory of God. (1 Cor. 10:31)

> And whatever you do, in word or deed, do everything in the name of the Lord Jesus, giving thanks to God the Father through him. (Col. 3:17)

To glorify God means to mirror or reflect his glory. Just as the stars in the sky shine brightly and show God's magnificent handiwork, so our work of obedience in all that we do points to the One who created us. We glorify God when we clean our house with a heart that is grateful for what the Lord has provided. We glorify him when we make healthy meals for our children's growing bodies, because we want to steward well what he has given us. We glorify him when we tell our children for the tenth time to look both ways before crossing the street, because we know how patient he is with us when we too are slow to learn. We glorify him when we are honest with our employers and when we smile at the cashier at the grocery store. When our hearts' desire is to do what honors and pleases God, when we want to show who he is by the way that we live out our lives, we give him glory.

All our work—whether we leave the house in the morning to go to work or work out of an office in our home or stay home to care for our children—is done for God's glory and fame, not

1. See the Westminster Larger and Shorter Catechisms, question and answer 1.

our own. It's done not for the praise or accolades of our boss or our children but for the sake of our Savior. Our hearts' posture is for Christ to be known—not ourselves. We want his name to be magnified throughout the earth—not our names.

When our work goes unnoticed, when our children seem indifferent to our labors on their behalf, when we do the same mind-numbing tasks over and over and wonder why it even matters, we need to remember for whom we toil. We live to honor and magnify the One who made us and saved us. All our work matters to God.

Christ's Work for Us

We can work hard at our mothering tasks because Christ first worked for us. His holy, perfect, and righteous work of obeying the law in our stead was given to us. "Because of him you are in Christ Jesus, who became to us wisdom from God, righteousness and sanctification and redemption" (1 Cor. 1:30). His sacrificial work on our behalf at the cross paid the penalty that we were due. "For our sake he made him to be sin who knew no sin, so that in him we might become the righteousness of God" (2 Cor. 5:21). Even now, he labors on our behalf before the throne and intercedes for us (see Rom. 8:34).

Jesus's work reshapes our own work and makes it holy. His work paves the way for all the work that we do—the seen and the unseen, the mundane and the spectacular, the boring and the interesting, the easy and the hard. Because of the work that Christ did for us, all our work is done through him and for him. Because we are united to him by faith, God looks at all our efforts and labors and doesn't see our failures, mistakes, blunders, and sins, but sees Jesus's perfect work on our behalf. When we are distracted by the chaos of motherhood and we get to the end of the day with the laundry still unfolded, Jesus's work covers our human frailties. When we get irritated with a child and raise our voices in anger, Jesus's work covers our sin. When we grow bored and discontented with life, Jesus's work covers that too. His work also covers our families when they overlook our efforts or take our work for granted or fail to show their gratitude.

In his grace, Jesus left us the Spirit who is at work in us even now, helping us in our labors.

> For the grace of God has appeared, bringing salvation for all people, training us to renounce ungodliness and worldly passions, and to live self-controlled, upright, and godly lives in the present age, waiting for our blessed hope, the appearing of the glory of our great God and Savior Jesus Christ, who gave himself for us to redeem us from all lawlessness and to purify for himself a people for his own possession who are zealous for good works. (Titus 2:11–14)

How amazing is God's grace for us in Christ! God not only saves us by grace, he also trains us through the Spirit by his grace. He teaches us how to live and work for him in this world. Consider what this means for our motherhood: God's grace is training us to put off our sinful desires and ungodly behavior and is helping us to be mothers who are self-controlled, upright, and godly. He is making us into moms who are zealous to do what is right and good. May we rejoice in the work Christ has done for us and marvel at the work he is doing *in* us, in this very moment, by his Spirit.

Our Work Is Never Wasted

When we are discouraged about the work we do as moms and wonder if our efforts are a waste, we need to remember that all things that are done for God's glory, and in his name, are never wasted. This includes the laundry we fold, the meals we prepare, and all the quiet, mundane acts of service we provide for our families. It includes our efforts to do the right thing when it would be easier not to. It includes working hard even when no one notices. It includes the prayers we pray ceaselessly with prostrate hearts. And it includes even the strings of words that lie dormant on my hard drive. All work that is done for God's sake is good work, whether anyone sees it or not.

God promises that our work for him will bear fruit.

> For the one who sows to his own flesh will from the flesh reap corruption, but the one who sows to the Spirit will from the Spirit reap eternal life. And let us not grow weary of doing good, for in due season we will reap, if we do not give up. So then, as we have opportunity, let us do good to everyone, and especially to those who are of the household of faith. (Gal. 6:8–10)

We'll see some of our work bear fruit in the here and now, but we may not see some of it bear fruit for years to come. We may not see our children use the table manners we've taught them at every meal until they are much older. We may never see their acts of kindness to other children on the playground. We may not see the fruit of our prayers for the Holy Spirit to work in their hearts for decades to come. But one day, in eternity, we'll see the entire tree—brimming and heavy-laden with fruit. We'll see how God used all our labors for his glory.

We are also assured that the work he is doing in and through us will be completed on his return: "I am sure of this, that he who began a good work in you will bring it to completion at the day of Jesus Christ" (Phil. 1:6). Our labor is imperfect, and we often make mistakes. We may wonder at times whether God is doing anything in us at all. But God always finishes what he starts. He will finish his work in us and make us like Christ. When our Lord returns, we will see the finished product and the result of all our efforts to serve and glorify him in this world.

Friend, in all your labors for the Lord, don't give up. Don't despair. All the work that you do for God's glory is storing up for you eternal treasures that far outweigh any accolades or acknowledgment you could receive in the here and now. None of it is wasted or lost. Your quiet faithfulness in all things, even in the unseen and the monotonous and the mundane, is seen by your Father in heaven. Let your Savior's holy and sacrificial work for you be the motivation and joy for your service.

For a Mom's Heart

1. Read Philippians 2:12–18. Who helps you to do the work that God calls you to do?
2. How can you glorify God in the mundane duties of motherhood? In your instruction? In your discipline?
3. Rejoice in prayer today that the Spirit is at work in you and that he never ceases that work until its completion at the day of Christ Jesus.

A Gospel Prayer for the Work of Motherhood

Therefore, my beloved brothers, be steadfast, immovable, always abounding in the work of the Lord, knowing that in the Lord your labor is not in vain. (1 Cor. 15:58)

Father in heaven,

I come to you, in prayer, exhausted from my labors. I don't even know what I have accomplished. I know that I met my children's needs. I know that I labored on behalf of my family. I know that I checked a few things off my to-do list—but then a few more things were added, too. But some days, my work for my children and family seems so monotonous. I repeat the same instructions over and over. I intervene in the same squabbles. I do the same task that I know I'll have to do again before the day is done. It's hard to think that this work matters—that my efforts make a difference.

But then I remember that you see all things. You know all things. You see and know all my labors—the big and small. Forgive me for forgetting that. Forgive me for living as though I work for the praise and affirmation of others, rather than for you and your glory. Forgive me for wanting to be seen by others rather than rejoicing that I am known and seen by the Maker of the universe.

I thank you for the work that Jesus did on my behalf. I thank you that all his work redeems my work and makes it holy. I thank you that you look at me and see Jesus's perfect life. I thank you for the Spirit's work in me that makes me more like Christ.

Help me each day as I nurture, teach, disciple, and care for the eternal souls you have given me. Help me to work hard. Help me to labor for your honor and praise. Help me to reflect you in my labors to my children and to others who see me. Help me not to grow discouraged or to give up in my labors. I pray that you would use my work to bear rich fruit for your kingdom.

Strengthen and sustain me by your grace. In Jesus's name, amen.

7

Even in Our Worries and Fears

O, how must God love that creature he has carried
so long in the womb of his eternal purpose!

WILLIAM GURNALL

One day my son walked into the kitchen and opened the refrigerator, searching for something to eat. I reached over and gave him a hug. "I love you. You know that, right?"

"Yes, Mom."

"How do you know that?"

"Because you worry about me," he said.

Out of all the responses a child could give to that question, that one surprised me. I expected something like "Because you always provide for me" or "Because you always look after me" or even "Because you tell me so every day."

What made him respond that way? Was it because I insisted that he pack a sweatshirt on his last Scout camping trip in case it got cold? Or because I barrage him with questions whenever he has a cough to determine whether it is asthma related? Or maybe it was because I remind him to drink plenty of water when he runs around outside. Or perhaps because I send him and his brother into public restrooms together? It may be that my son reads the worry etched on my face when he tells me that he doesn't feel well. It could be the way I respond when he struggles in school, sports, or friendships. Or maybe he can tell by my tone of voice when we talk about his future.

In his mind, my worry is a sign of my love. And, in many ways, it is. But just because my worries reflect a good thing— my love for him—it doesn't mean that they are a good thing in themselves.

The Worries of Motherhood

Moms worry; it's true. We worry about big things and little things. We worry about our children's health, development, friendships, education, and future. We worry about whether they're learning everything they should at school and whether it's safe for them to climb such a tall tree. We worry about strangers while they are playing at the park and about bullies while they are at school. We even worry that they will never function as adults and will need to live in our basements for the rest of their lives— after all, if they can't remember to brush their teeth each morning, how will they ever live on their own?!

All these worries point to important concerns. As moms, we have a responsibility to nurture and care for our children. We are to teach them certain things, protect them from harm, and provide what they need. We have specific duties to and responsibilities for our children that we need to carry out.

But sometimes those important concerns become worries that we dwell on. They fester in our minds and hearts. They keep us up at night and gnaw at us throughout the day. Such worry keeps us future focused—always thinking about and anticipating all the things that "might" happen. "What if?" is a constant question we mull over and over in our minds. We anticipate the worst: "What if _____ happens?" We consider every possible scenario and outcome and even strategize ways we can prevent whatever it is that we fear might happen.

These worries make us think that we aren't enough and haven't done enough. What if we aren't doing all we are supposed to do as moms? What if there's something big we've forgotten, overlooked, or failed to do? What if our children fail and it's our fault? Worry makes us compare ourselves and our children to others—makes us look for ways we haven't measured up.

Worry tells us that there's more to do. It makes us think we've missed something really important so that we lie awake trying to figure out what that is. We make lists. We can't rest until every item is crossed off the list. We research, plot, and plan—to the point that we are more prepared than any Boy Scout.

Are you a mom who worries? You are not alone. We all have fears. The truth is that we live in a fallen world where bad things do happen. Ever since Adam and Eve fell into sin, the entire world has been infected. The effect of sin touches every person; no one is immune. We are sinners who sin against one another. People sin against us. The creation itself is broken by the effects of the fall—by famine, disease, natural disasters, and more. Nothing works as it's supposed to. Everything breaks down and decays. We see evidence of the fall in the news all the time. It's not surprising that we would worry about ourselves and the ones we love.

The problem with worry is that it keeps our eyes fixed on what's happening in front of us (or even on what we think *might* happen) and not on the One who rules over all things. And ultimately, worry robs us of the joy and peace that is ours in Christ.

Do Not Worry

We're likely familiar with Jesus's admonition not to worry.

Therefore I tell you, do not be anxious about your life, what you will eat or what you will drink, nor about your body, what you will put on. Is not life more than food, and the body more than clothing? Look at the birds of the air: they neither sow nor reap nor gather into barns, and yet your heavenly Father feeds them. Are you not of more value than they? And which of you by being anxious can add a single hour to his span of life? And why are you anxious about clothing? Consider the lilies of the field, how they grow: they neither toil nor spin, yet I tell you, even Solomon in all his glory was not arrayed like one of these. But if God so clothes the grass of the field, which today is alive and tomorrow is thrown into the oven, will he not much more clothe you, O you of little faith? Therefore do not be anxious, saying, "What shall we eat?" or "What shall we drink?" or "What shall we wear?" For the Gentiles seek after all these things, and your heavenly Father knows that you need them all. But seek first the kingdom of God and his righteousness, and all these things will be added to you.

Therefore do not be anxious about tomorrow, for tomorrow will be anxious for itself. Sufficient for the day is its own trouble. (Matt. 6:25–34)

The Greek word that is translated in this passage as *anxiety* (or, in other translations, as *worry*) is *merimnáō*.[1] It is used to indicate something that divides, separates, or distracts. It means having a divided mind that is not working as a united whole. Worry

---

1. See James Strong, *The New Strong's Expanded Exhaustive Concordance of the Bible* (Nashville: Thomas Nelson, 2010), Strong's number 3309.

distracts us and pulls us away from what's important. We can't focus our attention on what we need to do, because our mind is consumed by all that we fear might happen. That's why we find ourselves up late at night thinking about our to-do lists and the "what if" questions. Our minds are distracted and divided. And the worry that this passage speaks of is not a passing concern; rather, it is a chronic habit—one that rules over us.

I used to read this passage as an impossible task—an unrealistic expectation. How could anyone not worry when their child is sick or is struggling in school or has trouble making friends? It seems inhuman not to be concerned about our children and their future—right?

Then I realized that this isn't a command given by a distant Ruler-King who doesn't know what life is like on earth. And this admonition is not like that 1980s song "Don't Worry, Be Happy." Such advice is trite and meaningless. After all, worry isn't something that you shut off in your mind by clicking the "be happy" switch. Fortunately, Jesus isn't telling us to do the impossible. Rather, this passage is a call from the very One who knows the end from the beginning, who created and sustains us, who holds the world in his hands, and who loves us and cares for our every need.

When Jesus tells us not to worry, he wants us to remember who God is and who we are. This passage is a reminder that it is God who gives us life. He is our Creator-God. Jesus tells us to look at the birds of the air and the flowers of the field to see how God cares for all his creation. Yet we are more than the animals. We are image bearers of our triune God. We are his vice-regents on this earth. If he provides for the flowers and the birds, how much more will he watch over and care for us?

As we consider Jesus's admonition in Matthew 6, we need to remember our compassionate Savior.

Our Compassionate Savior

Jesus, the second person of the Trinity, left the throne room of heaven and took on human flesh. He became like us in every way and yet was without sin. He experienced poverty and hunger, fears and sorrows, temptations and human frailty. He knows that this world is ravaged by sin and that there are real dangers here. He knows firsthand the evil in this world. He knows what people are capable of. He knows what it is to be human.

And, while Jesus is fully human, he is also fully God. He came to face all the things that we face and yet to live a perfect life. The book of Hebrews says this about Jesus Christ:

> Therefore he had to be made like his brothers in every respect, so that he might become a merciful and faithful high priest in the service of God, to make propitiation for the sins of the people. For because he himself has suffered when tempted, he is able to help those who are being tempted. (Heb. 2:17–18)

Jesus is our Great High Priest who goes before the Father and intercedes for us. Through faith in him, we receive Jesus's perfect life, sacrificial death, and triumphant resurrection. God looks at us and sees not our sin but Jesus's righteousness. Not only that, but all the times Jesus trusted and rested in the Father are credited to us. All the times he did not worry in the face of troubling or fearful circumstances are credited to us. Jesus's perfect trust in God is our perfect trust.

But that's not all. Because we are redeemed by the blood of Christ, we are adopted into the household of God. We call our Creator *Abba*. This is a close and affectionate name for a father— like the name *Daddy*. While our justification is a legal process through which we are made right with God, our adoption is about our relationship with God. We are now his children and are heirs of his promises. Now that God is our Father, we can trust him to provide for our needs. As the passage says, "Your heavenly Father knows that you need them all."

The Peace of God

How does this relate to the worries of motherhood? You might think that this passage is only talking about food and clothing. But Martyn Lloyd-Jones says, "It does not apply only to certain aspects of our life; it takes in the whole of life, our health, our strength, our success, what is going to happen to us—that which is our life in any shape or form. And equally it takes the body as a whole, and tells us that we must not be anxious about our clothing, or any of these things that are part and parcel of our life in this world."[2] All the cares of life—all the things that consume our minds with worry—we are to entrust into the hands of our Father in heaven.

Does this mean that when we entrust our cares into God's hands, the things that we worry about will never happen? No, that's not what it means. But God calls us to trust ourselves and our children to his care. He calls us to trust that, even if our children get sick or struggle or have trouble making friends, God is good and knows what is good for us. While we and our children will encounter hardships in life, God rules and reigns over those circumstances. We can place our hope in the promise that nothing and no one can separate us from the love of God in Christ (see Rom. 8:38–39).

Dear friend, Jesus doesn't want your mind to be divided over worries. He doesn't want you to be consumed by all the "what ifs" of life. He wants you to focus your mind and heart on his

2. D. Martyn Lloyd-Jones, *Studies in the Sermon on the Mount* (1959; repr., Grand Rapids: Eerdmans Publishing, 1976), 383.

kingdom: "Seek first the kingdom of God and his righteousness, and all these things will be added to you" (Matt. 6:33). He meets you with his sufficient grace right where you are—not in some far-off "what if" place, but in the very present moment. He meets you there with the truth of who he is and what he has done. He wants you to remember that you have a compassionate Savior who knows the worries and fears of life in a fallen world—so much so that he came to live and die for you.

What are we to do when worry comes knocking at our hearts? The apostle Paul echoed Jesus's sermon in Matthew 6 when he wrote,

> Rejoice in the Lord always; again I will say, rejoice. Let your reasonableness be known to everyone. The Lord is at hand; do not be anxious about anything, but in everything by prayer and supplication with thanksgiving let your requests be made known to God. And the peace of God, which surpasses all understanding, will guard your hearts and your minds in Christ Jesus. (Phil. 4:4–7)

Bring those worries to your Father in prayer—wrapped in thanksgiving. Come before him rejoicing in who he is and what he has done. Ask for help with and hope for your worries. Seek the One who knows all things—who knows the cries of your heart before you even give voice to them. Tell him your burdens, for he cares for you.

Paul tells us that God will then give us peace. What is that peace? Matthew Henry wrote, "The peace of God, that is, the comfortable sense of our reconciliation to God and interest in his favour, and the hope of the heavenly blessedness, and enjoyment of God hereafter, which passeth all understanding, is a great good than can be sufficiently valued or duly expressed. . . . This peace will keep our hearts and minds through Christ Jesus; it will keep us from sinning under our troubles, and from sinking under them; keep us calm and sedate, without discomposure of passion, and with inward satisfaction."[3]

This God-given peace is what our worried hearts need most. It's the peace that worry steals from us. My friend, let's seek that peace today.

For a Mom's Heart

1. Read Philippians 4:8–9. Rather than focus on the things that worry us, what should we focus our thoughts on?
2. What worries you today? What does the gospel have to say to those worries?
3. How would it change your parenting if your mind were less divided by worry? Does your worry ever take away from your time with your children?
4. Turn to God in prayer. Thank him for who he is and what he has done. Give him your worries and cares.

3. Matthew Henry, *Matthew Henry's Commentary on the Whole Bible* (Peabody, MA: Hendrickson Publishers, 1991), 2328.

A Gospel Prayer for the Worried Mom's Heart

*[Cast] all your anxieties on him, because
he cares for you. (1 Peter 5:7)*

Dear Father in heaven,

I come before you today with a heart filled with worry. I worry about my children. I worry about their future. I worry about harm coming to them. I worry about failing them as a mom. I worry about so many things. I find myself consumed by my worries. They keep me up at night, and I think about them all during the day.

So I come to you today because you are my Maker and Creator. You know my frame, my weaknesses, and my frailties. You know my inward thoughts. You know my sin. You know when a sparrow falls from the sky and know the number of hairs on my head. You know all things, and you also rule over all things. You are the King of Kings—the ruler of the universe. You sustain all things, and by your word everything is held together.

But you are not a distant ruler; you are my Abba—my Father. Through Christ, I have been adopted into your family. I have the privilege of coming before you, and you hear me. Because you are my Father, you don't want me to worry. I know that such worry is sinful because it keeps my heart distracted and turned from you. Forgive me for worrying. Forgive me for looking to my worries rather than seeking you. Forgive me for all the ways that I seek to control the things I worry about. Forgive me for trying to find peace in anything apart from you.

I know that you love me as much as you love your Son, Jesus. Help me to remember that and dwell on it. Help me to see just how much you love and provide for me—so much so that you gave me your Son. Help me to look at and truly see all the ways that you watch over and care for me and my family. Help me to rejoice in that and to give you thanks.

Hear my prayer today and all the cares that are on my heart. I entrust them into your hands, knowing that you will do what is good and right and best, for you are a good Father. Take my worries and give me your peace in return.

Because of Jesus I pray. Amen.

8

Fresh Mercy for a New Day

God's mercy and grace come directly from his heart, and run with a straight, direct, and natural stream. . . . What guilty, but broken heart, would not be encouraged to come to such a God?

Thomas Goodwin

"That's it! I've had enough! One more time, and _____!"

Have you ever said something like that? Your child or children wouldn't stop whatever you told them to stop doing, and you responded with something like the above statement. (Fill in the blank with whatever punishment you threatened.)

I've been there—more times than I care to count. Whether it was frustration over a child's tantrum in the grocery store or fatigue from debating with a teenager over whether my rules were fair or not, I've been stretched taut and ready to snap. In moments of frustration and anger, I've gone too far.

And then that feeling hits, deep in the pit of my stomach, as I realize what I've done. I've said something harsh and hurt my child. Or I've put them down with a string of sarcastic jabs.

Or I've overreacted and taken away a privilege for the next six months because I was so mad I couldn't think straight. I wish I had the power to pause time and rewind it to a few moments before I spoke. If only I could erase the past so that it never happened!

This desire is shared by all moms everywhere. Why? Because we've all responded in anger to our kids at some point. Perhaps we cut them to the quick with sarcasm. Maybe we were harsh in our discipline. We've all likely overreacted to childish behavior or expected more from our children than they were developmentally capable of and then, when they failed, were unkind in our response.

Sure, we may have had a reason. Perhaps we were tired or not feeling well. Maybe our child was extra challenging that day. Maybe she or he pushed our buttons just one too many times. Regardless of the circumstances, we sinned in our response. We realize that we ourselves were childish and handled a situation badly. Now we feel the weight of guilt pressing in on us.

In our regret and our guilty feelings, the gospel has something to say to us.

God Is at Work

That feeling of guilt—when we feel rotten for how we've treated our children—means that the Spirit is pricking our conscience and convicting us of sin. It means that God is at work in us, sanctifying us by his grace.

When we come to faith in Christ, we are washed clean of our sins and made new. God looks at us and sees Christ's righteousness, not our sins. But that doesn't mean that all of a sudden we are incapable of sin. It doesn't mean we are instantly perfect and do only what is good and right. While sin's power to hold us in bondage has been removed (see Rom. 6:6), the presence of sin still remains. We still have to put sin to death every day of our lives—until we die or Christ returns. Paul referred to this as "putting off our old self." He wrote to the Ephesians,

> Put off your old self, which belongs to your former manner of
> life and is corrupt through deceitful desires, and to be renewed
> in the spirit of your minds, and to put on the new self, created
> after the likeness of God in true righteousness and holiness.
> (Eph. 4:22–24)

The process of putting off sin (or, as the Puritans called it, "mortifying sin") is slow and tedious. It's more like a marathon than a race. We take steps forward and steps back. We stumble and fall and get back up again. It's not easy, and it's often downright hard. But it's a good and necessary process, because it's how God transforms us into the likeness of his Son. It's how we are sanctified—made holy.

When we feel the weight of our sin as moms, it's a good thing. God is doing a good work in us. He's showing us our sin so that we can repent of it, learn from it, and be changed by his grace.

Feelings of guilt remind us that there is a barrier between us and God. Our sin has lured us into the darkness, and we need to return to the light of God's presence. The psalmist felt the weight of his sin in Psalm 32. He wrote, "For when I kept silent, my bones wasted away through my groaning all day long. For day and night your hand was heavy upon me; my strength was dried up as by the heat of summer" (vv. 3–4). In Psalm 51, the psalmist likened the painful guilt of his sin to that of broken bones (see v. 8). In both psalms, he turned to God in repentance.

The Corinthian church also knew the weight of sin in their lives. The apostle Paul wrote a letter rebuking the Corinthian congregation for problems including sexual immorality, interpersonal conflicts, and theological confusion about various matters. This letter was stern, calling them to turn away from their immoral behavior and to reflect and glorify Christ. Paul sent Titus to deliver the letter and anxiously awaited the Corinthians' response. When Titus returned, he reported that Paul's letter had hit them hard. It had brought light to the dark corners of their hearts, and it hurt. They had responded to his letter with grief.

In a second letter, Paul referred to the grief that they felt over their sin as a "godly grief."

> For even if I made you grieve with my letter, I do not regret it—though I did regret it, for I see that that letter grieved you, though only for a while. As it is, I rejoice, not because you were grieved, but because you were grieved into repenting. For you felt a godly grief, so that you suffered no loss through us. (2 Cor. 7:8–9)

Their grief over sin pushed them to repentance.

And that's where our own guilt over sin ought to lead us, as well.

Repentance for Sin

When we've been angry and unkind to our children, when we've been harsh and unfair with them, when we've expected too much of them, we need to repent—both to the Lord and to our children.

First, we repent to the Lord because he's the one whom we've sinned against. All sin is against our holy and righteous God, first and foremost. God is our Maker and Creator; he is King and Ruler of all things. When we sin, we sin against him, and we must confess that sin.

We must cry out in prayer and tell the Lord what we have done and then ask for his forgiveness. It's not as though he needs to be informed of our sin; he knows all things. But when we repent of sin, we acknowledge and speak the truth. As Psalm 32:5 says, "I acknowledged my sin to you, and I did not cover my iniquity; I said, 'I will confess my transgressions to the LORD,' and you forgave the iniquity of my sin." The apostle John wrote that "if we confess our sins, he is faithful and just to forgive us our sins and to cleanse us from all unrighteousness" (1 John 1:9). What amazing grace!

In the famous list that he posted on the church door of Wittenberg, Martin Luther wrote that the Christian life is one of repentance. Every day we turn to God and confess our sins, appropriating what Christ did for us on the cross. We trust in Christ's righteousness to cover our sinfulness. We ask God to accept Christ's sacrifice for us.

Repentance doesn't only involve confession; it also includes turning away from our sin and turning toward what is right and holy. As J. I. Packer wrote, "Repenting means starting to live a new life."[1] That's what Paul referred to in the passage above when he instructed the Ephesians to "put on the new self." We turn away from what is sinful and turn toward what is holy. We pursue behaviors and attitudes and desires that are the opposite.

But we can't do it on our own. We need to seek the Holy Spirit's help in turning away from our sin. We pray for the fruit of the Spirit to grow and flourish in our hearts and to overflow into holy living. We trust and rely in God's work in us, not in our own strength. Though there is hard work for us to do as we put our sin to death and put on holiness, it ultimately happens because God is at work in us.

Therefore, my beloved, as you have always obeyed, so now, not only as in my presence but much more in my absence, work out

1. J. I. Packer, *Concise Theology: A Guide to Historic Christian Beliefs* (Carol Stream, IL: Tyndale Publishing, 1993), 162.

your own salvation with fear and trembling, for it is God who works in you, both to will and to work for his good pleasure. (Phil. 2:12–13)

Second, we must seek forgiveness from those whom we have hurt. We tell our children that we were wrong in our responses and actions, and we call our actions what they are: sin. Doing so means that we can't explain our behavior away by blaming our children in any way; we take responsibility for our own sins. We then ask for their forgiveness.

I tend to hurt my children with my words or my sarcastic tone of voice. The Spirit then pricks and convicts my heart. I repent of my sin to the Lord, and then I go to my children and say, "I am sorry for what I said to you. It was hurtful and wrong. Please forgive me." In doing so, I show my children the power of the gospel at work. My repentance reminds them that we are all sinners in need of a Savior—even their mom. It teaches them, by example, how to turn to the gospel for help and hope whenever they sin.

Abundant Mercy and Grace

Moms are going to sin. It's a guaranteed fact. We wake up feeling sick and have to trudge through the day. Perhaps our kids are sick as well. Maybe they are extra whiny or argumentative. Maybe they are slow to obey. We may be quick to frustration and anger. Or a child may go through a particularly challenging developmental season. We are at our wit's end about what to do. Our patience is diminishing fast. Or perhaps we simply want things to go our way; and, when they don't, we react in anger and our children receive the brunt of it. Whatever the circumstances, whatever the sin, there is good news.

God has an abundant supply of mercy and grace for us. In his mercy, God does not punish us as we deserve; in his grace, he shows us unmerited favor and kindness. We desperately need both! Throughout the Old Testament, God is described as loving, merciful, and faithful. It is part of his character; it is who he is. When God met with Moses on the mountain, he described himself as "the Lord, the Lord, a God merciful and gracious, slow to anger, and abounding in steadfast love and faithfulness, keeping steadfast love for thousands, forgiving iniquity and transgression and sin" (Ex. 34:6–7).

That's what the prophet in Lamentations reminded himself when he was going through a particularly trying and painful time. He remembered that God is a loving, merciful, and faithful God.

> The steadfast love of the Lord never ceases;
>> his mercies never come to an end;
> they are new every morning;
>> great is your faithfulness.
> "The Lord is my portion," says my soul,
>> "therefore I will hope in him." (Lam. 3:22–24)

In a discussion of God's mercy and faithfulness, Matthew Henry reminds us that, like Moses's burning bush, we are never consumed.[2] We may experience hardships, we may endure God's discipline, we may enter the refiner's fire, but we are never destroyed. Because God is merciful, because we are in Christ and he is our portion, we will endure.

At this time in redemptive history, we can trace God's mercy and grace throughout the pages of Scripture. We can see how he kept the covenant that he made with his people to be their God. We can see how he met our greatest need through the Redeemer who he promised way back in Genesis 3:15. We can see how he

---

2. Matthew Henry, *Matthew Henry's Commentary on the Whole Bible* (Peabody, MA: Hendrickson Publishers, 1991), 1330.

poured out his wrath on his Son so that we could be freed from sin and made right with God. Over and over, he showers us with mercy and grace.

This is good news when we have not been the moms we desire to be. It is good news when we see our sin in the shattered cry of a child at whom we've yelled. It is good news when we battle the same sin over and over. God isn't finished with us. He will not let us be consumed. His mercy and grace are without end.

For a Mom's Heart

1. Read Psalm 51. What can you learn from this psalm about sin, confession, and repentance?
2. Do you find the Spirit convicting you of sin? How have you responded to that conviction?
3. Turn to the Lord in prayer and confess your sins; acknowledge them to the Lord. Consider praying Psalm 51 aloud.

A Gospel Prayer for Repentance

*Create in me a clean heart, O God, and renew
a right spirit within me. (Ps. 51:10)*

Father in heaven,

I come before you feeling the weight of sin in my life. I was angry and yelled at the kids. Again. I used sarcasm like a lash that hit left and right. Their stunned and hurt expressions were like a punch in the gut that brought me back to reality. That made me see the truth of my sin. And that made me hate it.

As hard as it is for me to see the ugly truth about myself, I have to see the bad before I can embrace the good. I have to hate my sin before I can love your grace for me in Christ. Forgive me, Father, for my anger. Forgive me for taking out my problems on my kids. Forgive me for not being patient and kind and forbearing. Forgive me for excusing my sin.

I thank you, Jesus, for your sacrifice on the cross for my sins. I thank you for the great cost that you paid. I thank you for your perfect life that was lived for me. I thank you that you stand at the throne and intercede for me.

I thank you, Holy Spirit, for the work you are doing in me. I thank you that you are convicting me of sin and showing me my need for mercy and grace. I thank you that you are helping me to put off my old self and put on the new life that I have in Christ. Help me each day to mortify sin in my heart. Help me to be quick to repent. Help me to turn toward the things that glorify Christ.

I pray that, in spite of myself and my actions, you would be at work in my children's hearts. Help them to learn, from my sin, just how much we all need Jesus. Help them to love the gospel of grace and to seek repentance for their own sin.

Father, continue to shower your grace and mercy on me each new day. Help me to trust that your well will never run dry. Help me to draw from it instead of attempting to live by my own strength and resources.

I pray, along with David, "Create in me a clean heart and renew a right spirit within me."

In Jesus's name, amen.

9

Weary and Worn

This promise of spiritual rest is a promise left us by the Lord Jesus Christ in his last will and testament, as a precious legacy.

MATTHEW HENRY

Before I had children, my days were fairly predictable. I knew what to expect. I woke up promptly at 6 a.m., got ready for work, and left the house at the same time each morning. And though my work was challenging, my evenings and weekends gave me the opportunity for rest and relaxation before I returned to work again.

Life with children is different. Whether a mom works outside the house during the day or stays home with her children, there is no rest for the weary. While there is plenty of joy and sweetness in a mother's day, as she loves, nurtures, and cares for her children, motherhood can also be demanding and exhausting—physically, emotionally, and spiritually. There is no end to the work that needs to be done. There's no punch card to stamp at the end the of day. There are no shifts and no fifteen-minute breaks. There's no down time or vacations. A mom is always on duty.

Not only that, but a mom's work often seems harder than any other job she's ever had. The constant juggling of demands, the unexpected curveballs that children throw at her left and right, and the behavioral and discipline issues that pop up when she least expects it all keep her constantly on her toes. She often tries to anticipate what will happen next so she can be prepared (exploding diaper at a restaurant, anyone?). From discipline and training issues to caring for sick children, from answering countless questions to cleaning up another spill, from managing family life to rescuing a child who somehow climbed up on top of the cabinet, a mom's job would challenge and exhaust the finest brain surgeon.

While work is part of our pre-fall design—we were created for work—the physical, mental, emotional, and spiritual weariness that we sometimes feel, as a result of the overwhelming nature of our work, is not. We sometimes come to the end of ourselves, having exhausted our reserves so that we can't manage another thing. I don't know about you, but there are days when I find myself spent. It feels like I have nothing left to give. I've used up all my resources. I can't answer another question, solve another problem, referee another squabble, or produce another snack. I just can't.

We Need Rest

There's no doubt about it—motherhood leaves us weary. We know it. We feel it deep in our bones. We tell ourselves it will be better once the baby sleeps through the night or once the toddler gets used to sleeping in a "big kid bed" or once everyone's immune system matures so that they don't all catch the same bug all at once. . . . You get the picture. Sure, we'll likely sleep through the night once we no longer have babies to feed every three hours. But that doesn't mean there won't be bone-wearying days. In fact, as our children get older, we'll find ourselves staying up late so that we know they've returned home safely from an evening out with friends.

As moms, we are prone to take on every burden ourselves and

think that everything depends on us. We have high expectations for ourselves and try to stay on top of everything, whether it's having a spotless house and well-dressed children or keeping up with our volunteer duties at school or on the ball field. We follow behind everyone else in order to pick up the pieces and manage what was left undone. In addition to our motherhood duties, we have other responsibilities to manage. We live as though we are supermoms who are impervious to the boundaries and limits of human frailty.

When my kids were younger, I had to teach them what margins were on notebook paper. They automatically wrote all over the paper, ignoring the spaces at the top and the sides that they were supposed to leave empty. Such margins are put there for a reason. Imagine if you opened a book and found every inch of the pages covered in words. It would be overwhelming. We need those white spaces.

So it is with life. We need times of rest. We need margins in our lives.

Interestingly, it was before the fall that God designed margins of rest for us. It was before our bodies were broken and worn by the far-reaching tendrils of sin that God incorporated rest into his design for the world.

> And on the seventh day God finished his work that he had done, and he rested on the seventh day from all his work that he had done. So God blessed the seventh day and made it holy, because on it God rested from all his work that he had done in creation. (Gen. 2:2–3)

This Sabbath rest indicated that his work of creation was complete. He consecrated the day and made it holy.

After the fall, how much more do we need rest! We certainly need physical rest, for the stress of our labors wears on our bodies and takes its toll. We also need spiritual rest. And that's ultimately what the rest is that God incorporated into the creation order and commanded in the law. Such rest is grounded in finding peace in God and experiencing the joy of being in his presence. We experience this rest when we worship on the Lord's Day, remembering and celebrating who God is and what he has done.

But there's a greater rest that our weekly rest points to: *our rest in Christ.*

Christ, Our Rest

Jesus came to give us the ultimate rest that we need. He came to relieve us from striving to live life on our own—from trying to be the goddesses of our own kingdoms. He came to remove our burden of living as though life depended on us. He came to free us from trying to prove ourselves worthy to others and to God. He came to release us from trying to please him with our works and efforts. He came to relieve us from trying to save ourselves. He came to redeem us from our sin, to free us from our burdens, and to take on all our sorrows.

The Bible refers to our salvation as "rest." In Hebrews 3, the author compares Jesus to Moses, proclaiming him greater than the prophet who led the Israelites out of slavery. The author then uses the Israelites who wandered in the desert for forty years because of their unbelief as a negative example of those who did not respond to the "rest" or salvation that God provided. Quoting Psalm 95, he cautions his Christian readers,

> Today, if you hear his voice,
> do not harden your hearts as in the rebellion,
> on the day of testing in the wilderness,
> where your fathers put me to the test
> and saw my works for forty years.

> Therefore I was provoked with that generation,
> and said, "They always go astray in their heart;
>   they have not known my ways."
> As I swore in my wrath,
>   "They shall not enter my rest." (Heb. 3:7–11)

The exodus generation missed this rest. Even after they witnessed God's miraculous power and grace in the ten plagues, and even after he brought them through the Red Sea and defeated Pharaoh and his armies, they still did not believe. They grumbled and complained in the wilderness. They didn't trust God to be their rest and salvation. They thought that life in slavery would be better. They even created a golden calf to worship instead of the God who had proven himself faithful. Because of their unbelief, they did not enter his rest.

Since the writer to the Hebrews is showing how Jesus is better than Moses, he goes on to show his readers (and us) that there is a greater rest than the one found in the promised land: the rest that is found in Jesus. Hebrews 4:8–10 says,

> For if Joshua had given them rest, God would not have spoken of another day later on. So then, there remains a Sabbath rest for the people of God, for whoever has entered God's rest has also rested from his works as God did from his.

Through Christ, we cease our striving. We have rest in him and in his perfect life that was lived for us and his sacrificial death on the cross for our sins. We don't have to rely on ourselves to get everything right. We don't have to depend on our own strength to make life work. We don't have to walk around with guilt over all we have left undone.

Until Christ returns, the opportunity remains open for people to come to him and receive rest from their labors. But this rest comes only to those who trust in Christ by faith. It is not for the unbelieving. As Matthew Henry wrote,

> As sure as the unbelieving Jews fell in the wilderness, and never reached the promised land, so sure it is that unbelievers shall fall into destruction, and never reach heaven. As sure as Joshua, the great captain of the Jews, could not give them possession of Canaan because of their unbelief, notwithstanding his eminent valour and conduct, so sure it is that even Jesus himself, and captain of our salvation, notwithstanding all that fulness of grace and strength that dwells in him, will not, cannot, give to final unbelievers either spiritual or eternal rest: it remains only for the people of God; others by their sin abandon themselves to eternal restlessness.[1]

We have the benefits of rest now in this life and of a final, ultimate rest to come in eternity. This passage in Hebrews points ultimately to eternal rest in heaven, where we will stand before the throne of God with all the saints, from all time, and will marvel and worship at our great God and Savior Jesus Christ.

Rest Even in Chaos

It seems impossible for us to find any kind of rest in the season of motherhood—physical, mental, or even spiritual. With all the duties, responsibilities, and cares that we bear, it's hard to imagine having a single moment of rest to ourselves. Even at my stage of motherhood, with a tween and a teen in the house, I still cannot walk into the bathroom for even a minute without someone calling for me.

---

1. Matthew Henry, *Matthew Henry's Commentary on the Whole Bible* (Peabody, MA: Hendrickson Publishers, 1991), 2386.

When we can't even find physical rest, how can we expect to find spiritual rest as moms?

It can be tempting to give up on seeking our rest in Christ at this stage of life. We may think that life is too chaotic for us to find quiet time in our day to rest and focus on the Lord. But seeking such rest is not merely a matter of devoting an hour to Bible reading and prayer. It's not about having absolute quiet and focusing on God without a child in sight. It's not about developing a strict schedule by which we wake up at 5 a.m. to make sure that we have our devotions before the kids wake up—though these are all good ideas and worthy goals.

Rather, seeking rest in Christ is a posture of the heart. It's an all-the-time, 24/7 kind of thing. It's a constant state of the heart in which we are always leaning on the Lord and trusting in him to be our life and salvation. In truth, we can dwell on the gospel and what Christ has done for us even in the midst of the most chaotic day. We can turn to Christ for hope and strength no matter where we are and what we are doing. We can rehearse the gospel and feast on morsels of Scripture that are hidden in our hearts, even when we can't get to our Bibles. We can pray in our hearts to our Savior all throughout the day.

Taking hold of the rest that we have in Christ releases us from trying to carry the load of motherhood on our own. Remembering that we have a great Savior who bore all our sins and sorrows on the cross helps us to know that he cares about every moment of our motherhood. Even letting some things go and yielding our "supermom" expectations to God's hands means we trust that the Lord will structure our day and determine what is accomplished and what is not. When he, instead of a to-do list, becomes our focus, we can find joy in the busiest and most tiring of days.

Yes, we will be tired and weary during the season of motherhood—some days more so than others. But spiritual rest is always available to us. We don't have to live life as though it all depends on us. We don't have to be on top of everything, antici-pating every need, and solving every problem. We already have a Savior; we don't have to be saviors ourselves. So let us rest in who Jesus is for us. Let us rest in the salvation he's provided, knowing that we will experience it in full, in all its wonder and glory, in the world to come.

For a Mom's Heart

1. Read Luke 10:38–42. How was Martha missing out on peace and rest in Christ? Why did Jesus say, "Mary has chosen the good portion"?
2. It's true that motherhood is demanding and busy. It's hard for moms to find even a few minutes to themselves. How can you focus on your rest in Christ, even in the midst of chaos?
3. Pray and meditate on your rest in Christ today.

A Gospel Prayer for the
Mom Who Is Worn

Come to me, all who labor and are heavy laden,
and I will give you rest. (Matt. 11:28)

Dear Father in heaven,

I come before you weary and beaten down by this long day. Keeping up with work and life and my children's needs is sometimes exhausting. Everyone needs something from me, and all at the same time. I can't get a moment's rest. I feel weak and useless.

I do all I can to manage everything. I keep lists and try to anticipate what everyone needs. But just when I think things are moving along smoothly, someone gets sick. Or wakes me up because of a bad dream. Or goes through a particularly challenging developmental period. And then I'm reminded that I can't do it all. I'm reminded of my weakness and frailties.

And so I come to you to lay all these burdens at your feet. You are a good Father. You never grow tired or weary. Even while I sleep, you remain at work. You are never surprised or caught off guard. You are sovereign and all knowing. Nothing happens outside your knowledge and will.

Forgive me for trying to take on the world—for thinking I can do it all in my own strength. Forgive me for living as though I don't need a Savior. This long and weary day reminds me that I need Jesus more than I did yesterday and that tomorrow I'll need him even more.

Help me to rest and to rely on you. I pray that I

would find my confidence not in what I can do but in what you will do in me through Christ. Because of what Jesus did for me, I ask that you create in me a clean heart. Renew a refreshed spirit within me. Give me gospel strength to get through the day. Open my eyes so that I see your hand at work in the chaos of my life. Be my constant in the ups and downs of my days. Keep the gospel ever before me and make it a reality in my daily life as a mother.

I pray that tomorrow you would be with me in all the muck and mire of motherhood. Help me to find my peace and to rest in you no matter what is happening around me. May I remember that, even when it feels otherwise, you are always with me.

It's because of Jesus and in Jesus's name that I pray. Amen.

10

Who Am I?

If we could make ourselves, then we could live for ourselves. If we could be our own first cause, then we might be our own end. But God made us for himself, and sent us into the world for himself.

Thomas Manton

When I took my kids to see *Incredibles 2*, a movie short played before the main feature started. In this movie short, titled *Bao*, a Chinese mother struggles with being an empty nester. She is making dumplings one day and accidentally creates a dumpling that comes to life. She nurtures this baby dumpling and cares for it like a child. The movie shows her doing everything with the dumpling and often everything *for* the dumpling. We also see the dumpling go through all the stages of development, including the turbulent adolescent years. We see the mother resist her child's growing independence as he moves out and gets engaged.

At the end of the movie, my kids said, "What was that movie short even about?" I said, "Are you kidding me? It's about the heart of every mom." (As I sniffled and wiped tears from my face.)

A Life Poured Out

As I watched that brief movie, I saw many aspects of myself in the mother. It made me think about how I have lived my own life for my children. From their birth, I have spent myself for them. I have nurtured, fed, and cared for them. I have taught them and discipled them. I have read the same stories aloud over and over, played countless games of Battleship, and watched more Marvel movies than I care to count. I have stood and prayed over them when they were sick, nursed them through many an illness, and fretted through several surgeries. My days revolve around them and their schedules. In many ways, my life is about my children.

Recently, I've found myself asking older women what it's like to have an empty nest. It may seem a strange question to ask, because I still have eight or so years left before my youngest leaves home, but I ask it because I want to prepare my heart now. I think it's all too common for moms to wrap their identity up in their motherhood—so much so that their lives feel unanchored once their children leave.

We spend so much time and energy pouring into our kids that it's no wonder we are tempted to define ourselves by what we do as moms. It just hit me, at some point during the last few years, that I have a lot of extra time that I didn't have before. I find myself twiddling my thumbs in the evenings and wondering why I have nothing to do. Then I realized that I used to spend my evenings playing games and occupying the kids in some way. Now they go off together or by themselves and don't need me to entertain them. This is true of all stages of motherhood: little by little, our children grow less and less dependent on us. As they mature, they need us less and less. And if we find our meaning and purpose in life wrapped up in our motherhood, this is a hard truth to swallow.

But, on the flip side, there's another identity issue that moms often struggle with, and that is remembering who we used to be before we were moms. I don't know about you, but I used to identify myself by my work. When I met a new person, I used my job title as part of my description of who I was. I think this is true for most people. But then I pushed pause on that part of my life and jumped into motherhood. It was difficult to let that identity go. The work that I did gave me meaning and purpose— changing diapers and singing silly songs didn't, as much. I struggled with my new role and my new purpose. I kept asking myself, *Who am I?*

Work isn't the only thing from our past that often gets set aside. For some moms, the things that they enjoyed most in life get pushed out of the way. This might be a favorite hobby, an educational pursuit, or an athletic goal. We look back at our lives before motherhood and wonder, *Who is that woman and where did she go?*

Many things about our lives before we became moms were important to us—they shaped our days and fueled our goals. These things became part of our identity—but, when we took on the role of mom, they didn't fit so well anymore. We didn't have the time or energy to continue in them. Perhaps our finances changed, and we simply had to set aside our hobby or goal because of the added expenses of children. Maybe our previous interests just didn't make sense anymore. Whatever the reason, we may remember that part of our lives and feel grief over its loss.

All these things—motherhood, work, and goals or pursuits—are ways that we try to find meaning. They are what we use to try to find what defines us—our identity.

The Search for Meaning

We all search for identity—for meaning and purpose. We all need to know why we are here. We need a reason to get up in the morning and labor hard at our work. It's what gives shape to who we are. Identity is a good thing.

The world tells us that our identity is wrapped up in what we *do*. If we run, we are a runner. If we write, we are a writer. If we heal people, we are a doctor. If we teach, we are a teacher. If we have children, we're a mother. Whatever we do becomes our identity.

For the believer, though, there's another source that tells us who we are: God's Word. Scripture gives us an enduring meaning and purpose. It's something that will not change, no matter what changes in our lives or in the world around us. It won't change with our age or with the season of life we are in. It won't change whether we move to another town or join a different church or get another degree. It's not affected by what we do, but it does inform what we do.

The Bible tells us that when God spoke this world into existence, he created mankind. Our first parents, Adam and Eve, were made to image God.

> Then God said, "Let us make man in our image, after our likeness. And let them have dominion over the fish of the sea and over the birds of the heavens and over the livestock and over all the earth and over every creeping thing that creeps on the earth."
>
> So God created man in his own image,
> in the image of God he created him;
> male and female he created them. (Gen. 1:26–27)

They were given responsibility to rule over the world as God's representatives. They imaged him in all that they did: in their work, in their creativity, and in their rest. They glorified him in their obedience, in their relationship with each other, and in their enjoyment over being in God's presence.

Then they fell into sin. They defied the one thing that God

told them they couldn't do—they ate fruit from the forbidden tree. Because Adam was our representative, his action impacted us all. When he fell into sin, we all fell. We all inherit our sin nature from him. Yet even before God announced the curses upon Adam and Eve, he gave them this promise: "I will put enmity between you and the woman, and between your offspring and her offspring; he shall bruise your head, and you shall bruise his heel" (Gen. 3:15).

Jesus is the second Adam—the one who perfectly obeyed God and who is the fulfillment of that promise in Genesis 3:15. Jesus is God in the flesh, sent to redeem us and bring us back into right relationship with God. He came to restore what was broken in the fall. Through faith in his perfect life, sacrificial death, and triumphant resurrection, we are united to him and adopted into God's family. Christ's obedience is given to us—God looks at us and sees Jesus's righteousness. He gave us the gift of his Spirit, who is even now at work in us and is conforming us to the image of Christ.

What this means is that we were created as image bearers and made to reflect God's glory. Though his image in us was broken by the fall, through our adoption into the family of God we are now redeemed image bearers. That's our identity. We are "in Christ." We now live to bring him glory. The Westminster Catechisms tell us that our primary purpose is to glorify God and enjoy him forever.[1] That was Adam and Eve's purpose in the garden; and, through Christ, we are enabled once again to live out that purpose and identity.

When we wonder who we are in the various contexts and seasons of our lives, we have to remember this truth: *we are in Christ.* Whatever changes take place throughout the seasons of our lives,

---

1. See the Westminster Larger and Shorter Catechisms, question and answer 1.

whatever new experiences we face, we remain children of God. We are united with Christ; we bear his image in this world.

This identity gives shape to how we do the jobs, roles, and tasks that God gives us. It informs what it looks like for us to be wives, moms, friends, and coworkers. It defines how we serve and love others, and even how we live out the final years of our lives. This identity is always with us and will be with us into eternity.

What does the Bible say about being in Christ? It says many things, but here are just a few:

- *In Christ, we have forgiveness.* "In him we have redemption through his blood, the forgiveness of our trespasses, according to the riches of his grace" (Eph. 1:7).
- *In Christ, we are new creations.* "If anyone is in Christ, he is a new creation. The old has passed away; behold, the new has come" (2 Cor. 5:17).
- *In Christ, we are loved.* "I in them and you in me, that they may become perfectly one, so that the world may know that you sent me and loved them even as you loved me" (John 17:23).
- *In Christ, we were made for good works.* "For we are his workmanship, created in Christ Jesus for good works, which God prepared beforehand, that we should walk in them" (Eph. 2:10).

When I consider what life will be like without kids in the house, it's a little frightening—just as it was a little frightening to transition from work life to mom life. But my identity in Christ grounds me and gives me a meta-purpose that never leaves me, no matter what stage of life I am in.

As moms, we experience many seasons and stages in our lives. Some of us take off work for a brief season to have children and then return. Others may juggle both a demanding career and family life. Still others may work part-time throughout their child-rearing years. And some may never work outside the home at all but will spend their child-raising years at home with their children. No matter what we do with our time, it doesn't define us. No matter what tasks fill our day, no matter how significant they seem, no matter the joy that they bring us, they don't give our lives ultimate meaning and value.

What we do isn't who we are.

So who am I? Who are you? We are in Christ. We are God's own. We are daughters of the King. We are image bearers created to glorify and enjoy our Maker.

For a Mom's Heart

1. Read Colossians 2:6–15. What do you learn about your union with Christ?
2. Do you ever find your identity and purpose in your motherhood? What problems might this cause when your children need you less? Or when they don't appreciate your efforts for them? Or when they leave home?
3. Pray and reflect on who you are in Christ.

A Gospel Prayer for Moms to Remember Who We Are in Christ

But you are a chosen race, a royal priesthood, a holy nation, a people for his own possession, that you may proclaim the excellencies of him who called you out of darkness into his marvelous light. (1 Peter 2:9)

Dear Father,

Sometimes I just don't know who I am anymore. It seems like my identity and purpose are always changing. First I was a daughter and a student. Then I was an employee who worked hard at my job. I became a wife and struggled to navigate that new role. Now I am a mom, and I wonder how this all fits in with who I am and with my purpose in life. I'm often tempted to find my own value in what I do, and at the same time I wonder if I'm doing enough to matter.

Many things compete for my time and attention. My days are filled to the brim. I love being a mother, but it seems all-consuming. I do everything for my children. I anticipate their every need. I answer their every call. It seems as though I live my life for them.

Father, you have called me to be your daughter. You've united me to Christ by faith, and I am part of your family. You've given me an ultimate purpose: to glorify you and enjoy you forever. This is what gives my life meaning and direction. It's what shapes my days, my energies, and my time. As important as motherhood, or working, or anything else that I do might be, bearing your image in this world through my union with Christ is who I am.

Forgive me for seeking meaning and purpose outside of that. Forgive me for turning to my children for meaning. Forgive me for exalting my role as a mother far and above anything else. Forgive me for getting so wrapped up in motherhood that I neglect to glorify and enjoy you.

I pray, as my children move through their childhood and into adulthood, that I would live out my identity in Christ in all things. I pray that I would focus on your glory and fame and not on my own. I pray that I would honor and glorify you in my motherhood and in everything else that I do.

I thank you that I am your daughter. I thank you that I am in Christ. I thank you for all the benefits that I have in being part of your family and your kingdom.

Be glorified in and through me. In Jesus's name, amen.

11

Plans and Upside-Down Days

*Man can be very confident that God exercises the most
accurate providence over him and his affairs.*

Ezekiel Hopkins

We went on a trip to Disney World when my youngest was in preschool and planned to begin the drive after we picked him up from his half-day school program. When I arrived at his class, the teacher said he didn't seem to be feeling well. I buckled him up in his seat, and we headed to the land of dreams and fairy tales.

Except my son threw up in the car for the entire ride.

On another occasion, I drove eight hours to visit a friend and her kids in another state. We had fun visiting the beach and experiencing the food and culture of the Mississippi Gulf Coast. One day, we took all the kids to an indoor trampoline park, where they have trampolines even up the sides of the walls. The kids love these places. My friend and I found a quiet corner to relax while the kids jumped to their hearts' content.

Until my oldest came running up to me with blood pouring

out of his mouth and down his leg. While jumping, he'd slammed his teeth into his leg. His two front teeth were dangling by a thread—or rather a root. As I attempted to help my son while Googling a local emergency dentist, the owner of the trampoline park shoved forms in my face to sign, making sure that I wouldn't blame them for what had happened.

Needless to say, it was not what I had planned for our vacation.

I'm a planner by nature. I look ahead to potential catastrophes and plan accordingly. I'm the mom whose diaper bag always carried enough diapers to share, snacks to last a week, and toys in case of boredom. And today, though my diaper bag has been long since retired, my purse carries a small pouch with Band-Aids, cough drops, and antihistamines. Because you never know when you might get stung by a bee!

In spite of my efforts to be prepared, motherhood still throws me for a loop.

Unexpected and Upside-Down Days

Unexpected circumstances certainly cut into our days before we were mothers. Plans failed. At least once in our lives, we've had a flat tire on the way to somewhere important. We've come down sick and missed days of work. Maybe we've even had to stay overnight in the airport when a flight was cancelled. These are all frustrating events—uncomfortable and irritating, even. Yet such events are part of life.

But when you add little people to the mix, it seems that much harder. Am I right?

- The agony is compounded when your kid gets sick all over the grocery store floor—cleanup in aisle 9!
- The days are longer and harder when each kid passes on

their illness to another, and before you know it, it's been weeks since you left the house.

- The frustration only magnifies when you simply need to pick up milk at the convenience store and your toddler decides to have a meltdown in front of everyone.
- All you want to do is make dinner, but it's the witching hour, which means that everyone is on edge and fussing at once.
- You're at an important meeting with the principal of your child's school when the baby has a blowout—and you're out of diapers.

I'm sure we all have things to add to the list.

Motherhood is filled with unexpected and upside-down days, when our plans go awry and nothing goes right. I'm not talking about tragedies or disasters but about the everyday unexpected frustrations. Everything takes longer than it should. Nothing works right, and it seems like we are in a Monday-morning version of the movie *Groundhog Day*, reliving the same day over and over. Some days the chaos seems so ridiculous we can't help but laugh, and other days we want to bury ourselves in a hole and not come out until the kids turn thirty.

God Is on the Throne

All the chaos and unexpected events in our lives seem like they are random—a stream of bad luck. But the truth is that those upside-down days are governed by our sovereign, all-knowing, and all-powerful God.

God is the Maker and Creator of all things. He rules over all he has made, from the sparrows that fall from the sky to the hairs on our heads. He knows the number of our days and knows our thoughts before we even speak them. He sustains his creation, making the sun to shine and the rain to fall. He rules and reigns over the hearts of kings and determines the landing of the dice (see Prov. 21:1; 16:33). He determines all that happens, and nothing takes place outside of his will. "The Lord of hosts has sworn: 'As I have planned, so shall it be, and as I have purposed, so shall it stand'" (Isa. 14:24).

And though we make our plans, God directs our steps (see Prov. 16:9).

From small things to big things, God rules over and governs everything in our lives. Even the plans we make that are interrupted. Even irritating inconveniences, embarrassing mishaps, and unexpected challenges. He rules over our child's tantrum in the candy aisle, the rained-out park day, and the phone call that wakens the baby from her nap. As the Westminster Confession states, "God the great Creator of all things does uphold, direct, dispose, and govern all creatures, actions, and things, from the greatest even to the least, by His most wise and holy providence, according to His infallible foreknowledge, and the free and immutable counsel of His own will, to the praise of the glory of His wisdom, power, justice, goodness, and mercy."[1]

Not only is God sitting on the throne and determining all that takes place, he is also a good God. It is part of his character—he is good. "The Lord is righteous in all his ways and kind in all his works" (Ps. 145:17). He cannot do anything that is not good. "Every good gift and every perfect gift is from above, coming down from the Father of lights, with whom there is no variation or shadow due to change" (James 1:17). In spiritual terms, darkness implies evil; there is no darkness in God. He is the Father of lights, and he never changes. He is always good. As fallen creatures, we find it hard to fathom what that means. Even our good deeds are often tainted by wrong motives. But God always does

---

1. Westminster Confession of Faith, chapter 5.1.

what is right. He is the source of all that is good, and everything he gives us is good.

Our God is King. He reigns over all things; and because he is good, all his plans are good. They are right and just. While the difficult and trying circumstances that we experience may not be good in and of themselves, they are always used by God for his glory and our ultimate good (see Rom. 8:28–29).

Some people might resist this truth, but I find it to be a great comfort. When something crazy happens—like my son's accident at the trampoline court—I remind myself that while it may catch me off guard, it doesn't surprise God. He knew about it and willed it to happen. It was part of his good plan for my life and my son's life. The same is true for you: the exploding diaper, the round of sickness that doesn't seem to end, and the knock-down fight between siblings in the frozen food section are not random events in your life. God placed them there for a reason. And because God is in control over all things as King, because he is good, he has a good plan for our upside-down days.

Divine Opportunities

God doesn't place interruptions and unexpected events in our lives without a purpose; rather, he gives them to us in order to change us. Upside-down days are just another means by which God sanctifies us and transforms us into the likeness of his Son. While he does use big things, such as physical suffering or the loss of a job or even persecution, he also uses small things—seemingly random and insignificant things—for our sanctification.

Many of us don't experience a big, life-altering event that transforms our hearts in a profound way. Most of us are changed by the little things of life: the small decision to speak in kindness and love, the choice to invite a friend for coffee, the faithful act of making dinner each night for our families. It's the little things that shape us over a lifetime.

It's also those little things that become divine opportunities for us to face the reality of who we are and who God is. In truth, these inconveniences remind us that we are not God. They remind us that we are dependent creatures. They remind us that we don't have life all figured out, that we can't control what happens, and that we can't do life on our own. Our upside-down days then become opportunities for us to rely on God's grace and trust him for the strength to endure. They give us the opportunity to turn to the cross and remember our great need for a Savior.

These inconveniences also shine a light on our hearts so we can see what's really there: anger, self-righteousness, fear, and idolatry. They highlight sins that we have ignored or denied. They show us our desire to live as goddesses and queens over our own kingdoms. They reveal how we want to orchestrate things and how we desire for life to go our own way.

Those irritating interruptions and messed-up plans become opportunities for us to confess and turn from our sin. We can turn to the gospel of grace and find forgiveness. We can choose to obey God, to glorify him in how we respond, to honor him in what we say and do. And in so doing, we experience the Spirit's refining work in our lives.

We *need* upside-down days. We need those divinely orchestrated changes to our plans, because they open our eyes so that we see our need for Jesus—our only hope. Rather than resisting or avoiding upside-down days, we ought to embrace them, learn from them, and be changed by them.

For a Mom's Heart

1. Read Romans 5:1–11. What does it tell you about God's love for you? What do you have through Christ? What do you learn about God's work in your life?
2. Is it hard for you to look at the unexpected events of your days as divinely placed opportunities? Why or why not?
3. Pray for God to help you see his work in your life in all your upside-down days.

A Gospel Prayer for Upside-Down Days

We know that for those who love God all things
work together for good, for those who are called
according to his purpose. (Rom. 8:28)

Father in heaven,
     What a crazy week I've had! Everything has gone wrong. The kids are sick, everyone is grumpy, and I've had to cancel important things that I've put a lot of work into. This was the worst possible week for all this to happen!
     I'm angry and overwhelmed. I don't have time for all these interruptions. I don't have the energy or emotional bandwidth, either.
     But then your Spirit prompts my heart and reminds me that none of this took you by surprise. You weren't taken off guard. You knew that all this would happen. You reign over all things—right down to the fact that I ran out of milk just when I couldn't leave the house because everyone was sick.
     And when I ask myself why all this craziness has happened, I remember that you do all things well. You are a good God, and you do only what is good. As your child, who has been adopted in Christ, I will experience only your good for me. You desire not my happiness in the moment, but my holiness for all eternity. You are using each and every irritating moment and frustrating interruption to reshape me into the likeness of Christ. And sometimes that means cutting into my perfect plans for my day. Sometimes that means upside-down days.

Forgive me for forgetting who you are—the sovereign King. Forgive me for forgetting your goodness to me in Christ. Forgive me for acting like my kids do when I don't let them have any more candy. I know what is good for them, just as you know what is best for me. Forgive me for the way I have responded to these interruptions.

Help me to look at these upside-down days as sovereignly placed opportunities to glorify you and obey you. Help me to stop and ask myself, "What might God want me to learn in this?" Help me to find joy in the fact that I am your child and that you know exactly what I need. Help me to step back from staring at the inconvenience before me and to look at the big picture that you are painting.

I trust that you are for me.

In Jesus's name, amen.

12

Discontent in Motherhood

God is the highest good of the reasonable creature;
and the enjoyment of him is the only happiness
with which our souls can be satisfied.

JONATHAN EDWARDS

Have you ever gotten stuck on an "if-only"?

You know—that little phrase you whisper deep in your heart. That unspoken longing for something new, something bigger, something better. It's what we say to ourselves to explain why our lives aren't working. Our if-only is that one thing that would make life better and make us happier. It's the perfect shape to fit the hole in our heart, and once the if-only is in place we will feel whole and complete.

- If only my house were bigger, then we could invite people over and I wouldn't feel so lonely.
- If only my child would sleep through the night, then I'd be a better mom.

- If only we could have another child, then our marriage would get back on track.
- If only I had my pre-mom body back, then I'd feel better about myself and I wouldn't be so down all the time.
- If only my kids would listen, then I'd be a nicer mom.
- If only we had more money, then I wouldn't be so stressed and worried.
- If only . . .

One quick browse through social media, and the if-onlys take over. A scroll through the photos of other mom friends, and our thoughts immediately start wandering down the if-only trail. We start to wish that our lives were different. We start thinking that *if only* they measured up to our friends' lives. . . . We wonder, Why doesn't my home look like that? Why doesn't my child behave that way? Why doesn't my husband treat me special too? If only that happened, my life would be so much better.

We see photos from a friend's recent vacation and wish we were there. We read about a friend whose child achieved a big success at school or on the ball field and desire the same for our children. We see accounts of sweet things that children say or do and wonder why our children don't do the same. We read funny stories and think our own lives are jokes—but not the funny kind. We see the Pinterest-worthy crafts that other moms do and feel like failures. We see the elaborate, themed birthday parties that other moms host and declare that we are the worst moms in the world.

Social media gives us a peek into other people's lives and makes us think that our own lives pale in comparison. We forget that we're looking at a highlight reel that is carefully curated, even when the photo is chaotic.

But social media can't bear the blame; we compare ourselves to others in person, too. Such as when we meet up with a friend and hear about her latest trip or the amazing game that her child just played. Or when we visit a friend's house and see her child's recently redecorated bedroom. Or when we attend a playdate and see how many of the other babies have started walking, while our children are content to get everywhere on all fours.

Whatever comparisons we can make with those around us, whether virtually or in real life, we are drawn to making them. Our hearts are prone to seek out that one thing—that if-only—that we think will make our lives better and happier.

A Problem with Discontent

At the heart of our if-onlys lurks discontent. Our hearts are naturally discontent. From the moment our first parents listened to and believed Satan's lie—that their lives with God weren't good enough and that they needed to be like God—our hearts have been prone to wander. In our sin nature, we are prone to seek out life, hope, and joy in things, in circumstances, in experiences, in other people—anywhere else but in the One who made us.

We were created by God to love and worship him alone. We were made to know him and be known by him. But the fall of Adam and Eve led us to seek out counterfeit and false loves. We love and worship created things rather than the Creator himself. We seek hope, help, meaning, and worth outside of God. Because of this wandering nature in our hearts, we are easily discontent. We are restless and always searching. As St. Augustine once wrote, "You have made us for yourself, and our heart is restless until it rests in you."[1] We will continue to seek out if-onlys in our lives until we find our rest in God himself.

As believers, we know we are called to worship God alone.

---

1. St. Augustine, *Confessions*, trans. Henry Chadwick (New York: Oxford University Press, 1991), 3.

We wouldn't even consider bowing down to a statue made of wood, metal, or clay. And besides, we love God. We pray to him throughout the day and worship him on Sunday mornings. The reality, though, is that our if-onlys say otherwise. Our if-onlys say that God isn't enough—that we desire more. That we need more. So we add our if-onlys to our love of God. We worship him—and also the life we desire. We put our hope in him—and in a change in circumstances. But, as Jesus said, "No one can serve two masters" (Matt. 6:24).

God's people were guilty of this. We read account after account in the Old Testament of how God sent prophets to call the people to repent from looking for life and salvation outside of God.

> Be appalled, O heavens, at this;
>   be shocked, be utterly desolate,
>
>   declares the LORD,
> for my people have committed two evils:
> they have forsaken me,
>   the fountain of living waters,
> and hewed out cisterns for themselves,
>   broken cisterns that can hold no water. (Jer. 2:12–13)

Water is essential for life, and God is described as the source of all life; he is a fountain of living water. But Israel turned from God in order to create their own gods to worship. Their idols were like broken cisterns that couldn't hold water. Israel worshipped worthless idols that had no power or might to save them.

Discontent is idolatry. It's seeking life and hope outside the One who made us for himself. It's looking to something that has no power to save us and hoping that thing will make our lives work. And deep in our hearts, we know that it won't. We know that once we get that new thing, have that new experience, or receive that change in circumstance that we've long desired, we won't feel settled or content. We will just long for something else to fill the void.

The cure for our discontent doesn't lie in something new. It isn't found in some change. It doesn't come when our if-onlys are fulfilled. It's found in a person: Jesus Christ.

Content in Christ

Throughout his ministry, the apostle Paul had numerous near-death experiences, but also found himself in places of safety and security. Some days he had money to meet his needs, and other days he did not. In his letter to the church in Philippi, he thanked them for a gift they had given him that had helped to meet his needs. Out of the many churches he had started, this church had been the most generous and his most faithful financial supporter. As he thanked them, he wrote,

> Not that I am speaking of being in need, for I have learned in whatever situation I am to be content. I know how to be brought low, and I know how to abound. In any and every circumstance, I have learned the secret of facing plenty and hunger, abundance and need. (Phil. 4:11–12)

Some of us have read that passage many times and wonder how it's possible to be content in every situation. Such contentment feels out of reach.

We wonder, How can I be content when my husband travels all week and we barely spend time together as a family? How can I be content when my children struggle so much in school and no one seems to want to help? How can I be content when motherhood is so hard? How can I be content when I have a strong-willed child? Or one with special needs? Or one whom

I simply don't understand? How can I be content when I can't afford to give my children the childhood that I desire for them?

The secret to Paul's contentment in all his circumstances, whether he had plenty or had little, was that his heart was fixed on Christ. He explained his contentment to the Philippians: "I can do all things through him who strengthens me" (Phil. 4:13). Like Paul did, we need to root our own contentment in Christ, who he is, what he has done, and who we are because of it.

In Christ, we have all that we need or could ever desire. All those things that we look for in our if-onlys are found in him. In Christ, we find our meaning and purpose. In him, we find the help and hope that we desperately need. In him, we find perfect love. Christ fills all the voids in our hearts. He meets all our longings. He stills our restless hearts. Through his life, death, and resurrection, he provided for our greatest need—he restored our broken relationship with God. He restored our communion with God. Through Christ, we can once again know our Maker and Creator and be known by him.

> Blessed be the God and Father of our Lord Jesus Christ! According to his great mercy, he has caused us to be born again to a living hope through the resurrection of Jesus Christ from the dead, to an inheritance that is imperishable, undefiled, and unfading, kept in heaven for you, who by God's power are being guarded through faith for a salvation ready to be revealed in the last time. (1 Peter 1:3–5)

Did you catch that? Our hope is a living hope that is secured for us through Christ's resurrection. Because he conquered the grave, we have the hope of eternity.

Like Paul, we need to look to Christ as our source of contentment and joy. We must continually strive for and seek after him. Though we are redeemed, we continue to sin. Our hearts still wander. Therefore, we must abide in Christ. We do so by communing with him through his Word and through prayer, by depending and relying on his grace in all things, by worshipping together with the gathered saints. And the more we abide in Christ, the more our hearts are surgically transformed by his living and powerful Word. The more his Word shapes us, the more our longings and hopes conform to his will, and the more we find ourselves content with whatever circumstances the Lord provides. The more we find our contentment in Christ, the weaker our if-onlys become and the more we love what God loves.

And then, like Paul, we can say that we have learned to be content whatever our circumstances. Because real joy is not dependent on what happens in our lives and/or our motherhood. It's not dependent on whether our children take a nap each day or get into the schools we wanted or get a certain score on a test. It's not dependent on what we have or don't have, how others treat us or don't treat us, or even whether we meet the goal we are pursuing. Circumstances come and go, but real joy is bound up in something that doesn't change. It's grounded in what we have in Christ. And that's something that will never change. This joy remains with us even in hard times. It doesn't flee in face of grief or loss. It walks alongside our worries and fears. It's a steady undercurrent that carries us through the storms of life.

When we find that our hearts are discontent and we long for something new and better and we begin to look for it in all the wrong places, we need to cry out to God. Not to ask him to make our lives better but to ask for a clean heart. We need to seek him in repentance and apply to our lives and hearts what Christ has done for us in the gospel. We need to abide in him and to remember that apart from him we can do nothing.

Then the thing that we ask for won't be what our neighbor has. It won't be a change in circumstance. It won't be a plea for something new or better. Rather, we'll be able to say with the psalmist, "One thing have I asked of the LORD, that will I seek after: that I may dwell in the house of the LORD all the days of my life, to gaze upon the beauty of the LORD and to inquire in his temple" (Ps. 27:4).

For a Mom's Heart

1. Read Psalm 27. David had a number of problems in his life. How could he say that the one thing he wanted was to be in God's presence? What are some words he uses in this psalm to describe God? On this side of redemption, how do we see verse 1 fulfilled in Christ?
2. What is your if-only? What do you look for, outside of Christ, to give you hope in your motherhood?
3. Turn to the Lord in prayer. Repent of the idols you worship. Seek your joy in who Christ is and what he has done.

A Gospel Prayer for the Discontented Heart

Therefore, since we have been justified by faith, we have peace with God through our Lord Jesus Christ. Through him we have also obtained access by faith into this grace in which we stand, and we rejoice in hope of the glory of God. (Rom. 5:1–2)

Dear Father in heaven,

I come before you longing for a change in my life. Motherhood is not what I thought it would be, and I need things to change. Lately, I find myself thinking, "If only _____ happened, then my life would be better. I'd be happier. I'd be content in motherhood."

Even as I pray these words, I see them for what they are: an attempt to find hope and life outside of you. My discontent reveals idols in my heart. I know I am prone to worship false gods. I am prone to look to circumstances or things or people to meet the needs that only you can provide. Forgive me for my idolatrous heart. Forgive me for thinking that what I need most is a change in circumstance, when what I really need is you.

You are my Maker and Creator. You know me inside and out. You created me for yourself—to worship, love, and honor you. Whenever I look to idols, I fail to give you the honor you deserve. I steal your glory from you and attempt to give it away.

Help me to see the weakness and powerlessness of the things I cling to. Help me to see that my if-onlys will not make my life better or happier. They cannot fill the void in my heart. Only you can.

I thank you for Jesus, who redeemed me from sin with his blood so that I can be in right relationship with you again. I thank you for his resurrection from the grave, which secured for me an eternal hope—a living hope. I thank you for the joy that I have in him—a joy that can't be taken away.

Help me to look for and long for that final day when my hope will be revealed.

In Jesus's name, amen.

13

When Our Children Sin

You cannot make your children love the Bible, I allow. None but the Holy Ghost can give us a heart to delight in the Word.

J. C. RYLE

Children are a delight and gift from the Lord. "Behold, children are a heritage from the LORD, the fruit of the womb a reward" (Ps. 127:3). When we first learn that we will have a child, we pray over our little one day after day. Even though we've never met him or her in person, we love our child more than anything. We wait for months—and, for adoptive moms, sometimes years—in anticipation of the amazing moment when we will hold that precious gift of God in our arms.

When our children are first born, or first placed in our arms by an adoption agency, it can be hard to think of those sweet babies as sinners (unless they cry all night—then we are convinced of it!). It isn't until our precious little ones start to move around, begin getting into things, and even start to talk back that the evidence of their sinfulness hits us. That first time they reach out to touch something right after we've told them not to, or the first time they yell "No!" in response to an instruction we've given them, the truth that we've known in our minds all along about their sinful state is fully realized. The doctrine of sin that we learned in church hits us square in the face: our children inherited the same sinful state that we all inherit from Adam.

As the Westminster Confession teaches us,

> Our first parents being seduced by the subtilty and temptation of Satan, sinned in eating the forbidden fruit. This their sin God was pleased, according to his wise and holy counsel, to permit, having purposed to order it to his own glory.
>
> By this sin they fell from their original righteousness and communion with God, and so became dead in sin, and wholly defined in all the faculties and parts of soul and body.
>
> They being the root of all mankind, the guilt of this sin was imputed, and the same death in sin and corrupted nature conveyed to all their posterity, descending from them by ordinary generation.[1]

Our children don't become sinners after they commit their first sin; they are sinners starting from the time they are conceived. As David wrote, "Behold, I was brought forth in iniquity, and in sin did my mother conceive me" (Ps. 51:5).

Even though we have this theological knowledge, it's sometimes shocking to see our children's sin on full display: angry outbursts, lying, stealing, idolatry, bullying, and defiance, to name a few. And all this can happen before a child enters kindergarten! As our children grow into their teen years, they will face still greater temptations to sin. More than being shocking, it's often disheartening to watch our children sin. It can break our hearts when our children make choices that lead them farther and farther off the path of life. Many a mom has wept over her child's sinfulness.

Take a moment to consider the sins you have committed in

---

1. Westminster Confession of Faith, chapters 6.1–3.

your life—particularly those that you committed in your youth. I don't know about you, but I don't want my children falling into some of the same sins that I did in my past. I definitely don't want them to pursue sins that will hurt them and others around them. But the reality is that our children will sin. The sins they commit may be similar to ours, or they may be different. The natural consequences that they experience may be worse than ones we have faced, or they might not. We have to remember that even if our children don't pursue sins that our society considers the most shameful or destructive, whatever sins they commit are still committed against a holy and righteous God. They are still serious. Perhaps rather than being outwardly rebellious, our children may be prideful and self-righteous. Instead of worshipping the accolades of peers, they might worship knowledge or technology. They might not commit grand sins that get them in trouble everywhere they go; their sins might be more internal—in their thoughts or beliefs.

Whatever the sins our children struggle with in their lives, they need a Savior just as much as we do.

Our Children's Greatest Need

Before I had children, I worked as a child psychotherapist. I often taught parenting skills as part of my responsibilities. When I met with parents to talk about their parenting, I often started off by talking about the overall philosophy and goals of parenting. I wanted them to look at the big picture first before we narrowed in on any kind of method. But the parents I met with did not want to discuss the philosophy of parenting. They just wanted to know how to get their children's behavior to stop. They'd say to me, "Just tell me what to do to get my child to stop _____."

While there are good and helpful things we can do to help our children with their sinful behavior, such as providing structure and routines, being consistent in our expectations and discipline, and making sure that they eat well and get plenty of rest, ultimately what our children need is a new heart. Because at the heart of our children's sinful behavior is a heart problem; at the heart of the matter is the heart.

Why the heart? Because the heart is the core of who we are as humans. When the Bible talks about the heart, it doesn't mean our physical heart—the one that pumps blood throughout our bodies and keeps us alive. It also isn't referring to the heart-shaped confections and cards that we give to those we love on Valentine's Day. The Bible uses the word *heart* to mean our inner self—who we are as a person—the real us. This inner self includes our thoughts, our desires, our feelings, our personality, our motives and intentions, and the choices we make. As it says in Proverbs, "As in water face reflects face, so the heart of man reflects the man" (Prov. 27:19) and "Keep your heart with all vigilance, for from it flow the springs of life" (Prov. 4:23).

Because we are fallen, like all of mankind, our hearts are prone to sin. What we need is a new heart—one that is able to love and obey God. This is what God promised in the book of Ezekiel.

> And I will give them one heart, and a new spirit I will put within them. I will remove the heart of stone from their flesh and give them a heart of flesh, that they may walk in my statutes and keep my rules and obey them. And they shall be my people, and I will be their God. (Ezek. 11:19–20)

This is what the Holy Spirit does when he awakens our dead hearts to life. Theologians call this awakening *regeneration*. The Spirit gives us a new heart—one that is capable of responding to God in faith. "But God, being rich in mercy, because of the great love with which he loved us, even when we were dead in our trespasses, made us alive together with Christ" (Eph. 2:4–5).

What our children need most isn't help with stopping an unwanted behavior or sin, but a new heart. They need the Spirit to bring them from death to life. They need their eyes to be opened to spiritual truth so that they can see their need for Jesus and what he did for them in his life, death, resurrection, and ascension. They need the gift of faith so that they can turn to Christ and receive salvation and forgiveness of sins. They need the Spirit to work in them—to sanctify them and transform them into the likeness of Christ.

Preach, Point, and Pray

When we see our children sin, whether they are young toddlers touching breakables on the shelf or first graders lying about a school assignment or teens watching a movie they are forbidden to watch, we need to remember the gospel. When we despair over our children's choices, we need to remember the gospel. When we fear the path that they are headed down, we need to remember the gospel.

We need to preach the gospel to ourselves—to remember that we are all born fallen in sin. We ourselves were once separated from God, and it was by his grace that he saved us. We must remember that our children need the same gospel that we need. It's not going to be our excellent parenting or a top-notch education or amazing life experiences that transform our children; rather, it's going to be the power of the gospel. We have to trust and look for God to work in their hearts and lives.

We also need to point our children to the gospel. We have a responsibility as parents to teach and disciple them in the faith. As the Lord says in Deuteronomy 6:6–9,

And these words that I command you today shall be on your heart. You shall teach them diligently to your children, and shall

talk of them when you sit in your house, and when you walk by
the way, and when you lie down, and when you rise. You shall
bind them as a sign on your hand, and they shall be as frontlets
between your eyes. You shall write them on the doorposts of
your house and on your gates.

On this side of the history of redemption, we need to teach
our children who Jesus is and what he came to do. We need to
teach them about the perfect life he lived for them, his sacrificial death, his triumphant resurrection from the grave, and his
ascension back into heaven. The gospel is the story that we tell
them when they sit, when they walk along the way, when they lie
down, and when they rise. At all times and in all places, we point
our children to the gospel. While it is the Spirit who brings our
children from death to life, we parents are one of the means that
God uses to save our children. Perhaps this could be compared to
how God uses our prayers to carry out his will—he doesn't need
to, but he chooses to. This truth should compel us all the more
to be diligent in our labors to teach and instruct our children in
God's Word.

Finally, we need to pray for the Lord to work in our children's
hearts. As moms, it's easy for us to focus our prayers on the health
of our children or on their success in school. We may find ourselves praying that they would develop good friendships or that
they wouldn't be bullied on the playground. We may even pray that
they would stop fighting with their siblings or having tantrums.
These are all excellent and important prayers. But the prayer that
we can't forget to pray is that God would ratify his covenant in our
children's hearts. We must pray that he would save our children
from their sins.

The apostle Paul wrote a number of prayers in his letters to
the churches he served. These prayers don't mention their physical needs. They don't mention the believers having a roof over

their head or recovering from a cold—though perhaps Paul did pray those things. (Jesus taught us to pray for our daily needs in Matthew 6:11). His prayers centered around their hearts. He prayed for God to transform them through his grace. He prayed that they would grow in their love and knowledge of God. The prayers that he prayed for them were focused not on the temporary but on the eternal. He prayed for the work of the kingdom and the spread of the gospel through them. He prayed for their spiritual strength and encouraged them with the hope that they had in Christ because of his perfect life and sacrificial death.

Here is an example of one of those prayers:

> For this reason I bow my knees before the Father, from whom every family in heaven and on earth is named, that according to the riches of his glory he may grant you to be strengthened with power through his Spirit in your inner being, so that Christ may dwell in your hearts through faith—that you, being rooted and grounded in love, may have strength to comprehend with all the saints what is the breadth and length and height and depth, and to know the love of Christ that surpasses knowledge, that you may be filled with all the fullness of God. (Eph. 3:14–19)

May we moms pray such prayers for our children: that God would open the eyes of their hearts, that they would see their need for him, that they would respond in faith to the gospel, that they would be transformed into the image of their Savior.

For a Mom's Heart

1. Read the prayers of Paul: Ephesians 1:17–19; 3:14–19; Philippians 1:9–11; Colossians 1:9–11; 1 Thessalonians 5:23–24. In what ways does he refer to the gospel? What

do you learn from these prayers that can shape your own prayers for your children?

2. How do you respond to your children's sin? Are you surprised? Disheartened or discouraged? Fearful?

3. Turn to God in prayer and pray one of Paul's prayers— both for yourself and your children.

A Gospel Prayer for Our Children's Hearts

He established a testimony in Jacob and appointed a law in Israel, which he commanded our fathers to teach to their children, that the next generation might know them, the children yet unborn, and arise and tell them to their children, so that they should set their hope in God and not forget the works of God, but keep his commandments. (Ps. 78:5–7)

Father in heaven,

I come to you today with a burdened heart. A weary heart. A heavy heart. Parenting is hard. Just when I think I know what I'm doing, something changes, and I need to learn something new. Some days I wonder if I'll ever feel confident in my parenting. But maybe that's the point. Maybe I'm not supposed to be confident in my methods and strategies. Maybe those methods aren't always supposed to "work." Maybe parenting is supposed to keep me on my toes because, instead of trusting in what I am doing as a parent, I need to trust in you. Maybe parenting is hard so that I will learn to depend and rely on you and on your Spirit to be at work in my life and in the lives of my children.

Father, I bring my children before you. They are covenant children who enjoy all the rich benefits of being part of the church, of hearing the Word preached each week, of having other adults pour into their lives, of learning and memorizing your Word. I pray that you would ratify the covenant in them. Bring them from death to life by the power of your Spirit. Open their minds and hearts to see their need for Jesus. Convict them of sin and draw them to repentance. Help them to love you with all their heart, mind, soul, and strength. Be at work in them, refining and shaping them into the image of Christ. Protect their minds and hearts from evil, and may they never know a day when they did not know you as Lord of their lives. May Jesus always be their greatest treasure.

I pray for my parenting decisions and responses. Help me to parent out of your wisdom and not my own. Help me to seek your glory and not my own. Help me to speak the truth in love, point my children to Christ, teach and discipline them according to your Word, and love them as you have loved me. Help me not to fret, worry, or fear. Help me not to despair. Help me not to overreact. Help me to remember that they are sinners, just as I am. Help me to remember that they need a Savior, just as I do. Help me to trust and rest in you and in the power of the gospel at work—in me and in them. Help me to be quick to repent, slow to anger, and generous with love and affection.

Good things happen while we wait. It took time for these precious souls to be knitted in my womb—what joy I felt at their arrival! May I be patient as I wait for the work you are doing in their hearts. Help me to watch and wait with hope and trust. Help me to see and trace the evidence of your grace at work in their hearts. Help me to glory in your goodness and faithfulness in Christ.

Please hear all these cries of my heart. In Jesus's name I pray, amen.

14

When Motherhood Is Lonely

You have had many trials and troubles; has he ever deserted you? . . . No, children of God, it is your solemn duty to say "No," and bear witness to his faithfulness.

C. H. Spurgeon

My husband often travels for work; and, when my children were young, I often joined forces with other moms whose husbands also traveled for work. We would take turns hosting each other for dinner, meeting at a kid-friendly restaurant, or bringing a picnic to the park. Sometimes, when my husband was out of town and another friend's husband was in town, she would come over in the evening and keep me company. We'd watch chick flicks together and do a "dark chocolate tasting."

Though we have little people in our homes with us, motherhood can often be lonely and isolating. Such loneliness looks different for every mom. Some have husbands who work long hours or travel for days at a time, and they simply want another adult to talk to. After answering question after question of "Why" this and "How" that, moms are desperate to talk to anyone taller than three feet.

Other moms may have just moved to a new town where they don't know a single soul. They don't have any family nearby, and there's no one to help with the kids. There's no one who knows and cares for them.

Some moms have a child with unique challenges or needs, and they may feel isolated from other moms whose children don't have such challenges. Their lives may revolve around their child's unique needs. Their days may be spent at doctors' offices or specialists. Perhaps they don't have the time to meet up with other moms for story time at the library or for an afternoon of play at the local children's museum. Their circumstances may make it difficult for them to connect with others. They may not know many other moms who are in similar circumstances.

And still other moms are completely on their own in parenting, with no husband to help them bear the burden. They have to do it all. They feel the weight of the responsibility of handling discipline and other parenting duties on their own. There's no one for them to pass it off to. Not only that, but their days are filled to the brim, leaving no time for friendship.

Particular seasons of motherhood can be lonelier than others. There are many opportunities available for moms to spend time with other moms when children are little. There are mommy-and-me classes, story time at the library, Bible studies for young moms, playgroups, and the like. This season provides necessary time for moms to have other people to connect with and to share the joys and challenges of motherhood. But then the kids start school and some of the moms who were staying at home with their littles return to work. Life gets busier, and they miss the time that they had with other moms.

Even as children get further into their school years, motherhood can be lonely. They are at school all day, and moms may work during that time, manage responsibilities at home, or volunteer at their children's schools. Some may spend their days homeschooling. Once the school day is over, moms are kept busy with homework and with driving each child to whatever activity they are involved in. Weekends are busy with sports and family obligations. All this activity can make it challenging to find time for friendship and connection with others.

Indeed, motherhood can be quite lonely.

Created for Community

That feeling of loneliness isn't something to be ignored or minimized. It isn't something to overlook or pretend away. We have those feelings because we were made to be in community; God didn't create us to live life on our own. When God created Adam from the dust of the earth, he made him to be an image bearer—to reflect God in all that he was. Because God is a triune community of Father, Son, and Holy Spirit, Adam needed someone else to live with in community. "It is not good that the man should be alone" (Gen. 2:18). So God created Eve. Together, they reflected God in community with each other. And when we honor, serve, and love others in the context of community, we too reflect our Maker.

Throughout the Scriptures, we see God working through communities. He made a covenant with Abram to make him a father of many nations. He called his covenant children out from slavery in Egypt and brought them to the promised land. Through Christ, he created the church—a body of believers who are united through the blood of Christ. "Now you are the body of Christ and individually members of it" (1 Cor. 12:27).

God works through the community of the church to build up and establish his kingdom. He uses each of us in the lives of other believers so that we bless, encourage, exhort, and urge one another on in the faith. Over and over in Scripture, we see the writers commanding us to love and serve one another. To bear one another's burdens. To urge one another on to love and good deeds. To lament and mourn with one another. To teach and train one another in the gospel. This means that we need community. We need Christian community. We need the church.

As moms, we need the family of Christ to pour into us out of the overflow of the Spirit's work in them. We need their gospel encouragement when we are overwhelmed and discouraged by motherhood. We need them to walk alongside us in the journey, point us forward when we lose our way, urge us back onto the path when we wander, and pick us up when we stumble. We need other moms who understand the stage of motherhood we are in and will help us through it. We need older moms who can disciple us in how to live out the gospel in our motherhood. We need brothers and sisters who will help us in practical ways when we can't help ourselves. In all these ways and more, we need Christian community.

When we feel lonely as moms, that loneliness serves as a reminder to us that we were not meant to be lone rangers. We were made to be a part of a greater community—to help, serve, and love others in the family of God. When we feel that loneliness, it means there's a barrier of some kind between us and our family members in Christ. That barrier might be different for me than it is for you. We need to consider what that barrier might be and to seek the Lord's help in overcoming it.

One way to do so is to pursue community with others.

Pursuing Community

Whatever our life circumstance, whatever season of motherhood we are in, whatever our loneliness looks like, it is important that we try to stay connected. We need to be intentional in seeking out community in the body of Christ. We need to seize opportunities when they come and create them when they don't. Loneliness will not get better unless we do something about it.

What might this look like?

- *Invite other moms over for a playdate.* If you are a stay-at-home mom and have your days available, create a playgroup for other moms from your church. Meet each week and encourage one another in your mothering.
- *Invite singles to your home for meals and holidays.* You may think that your home life is chaotic and overwhelming, but there are many brothers and sisters in the church who would love to enter the chaos and be welcomed in as part of your family. This benefits your children, as well, as they learn to practice hospitality.
- *Meet other women for coffee.* Whether you work during the day or not, there are always evenings and weekends. Consider meeting another woman or two for coffee regularly so you can talk and share about your life.
- *Read a Christian book together with an older woman in the church.* There is much we can learn from older women in our churches. Even if you can't get together with someone like this weekly to talk about what you have read, send her a text message or email with your thoughts and responses. Share prayer requests with her and try to meet regularly to pray with her.
- *Attend Bible study.* Many churches offer Bible studies at different times of the day to meet the schedule needs of their members. Learning God's Word with other believers is an essential part of Christian community. Hearing other people share what they are learning from Scripture opens our own eyes to things we hadn't noticed before. We learn through what others learn, and they learn through us.

- *Notice those on the outside.* Some of the best opportunities for community can come from meeting someone new— someone on the outside. Look for those who don't participate much in church activities, and try to reach out to them. Find out about their lives and their stories. Seek to involve them in community.
- *Look for holes in community.* Are there several moms with special-needs children in your church? Consider bringing them all together for encouragement. Are there single moms in your church? How can they be included in community? What about widows and widowers?

Never Alone

At times, we are alone for a season and there is little we can do to change it. Perhaps we've recently moved to a new place and will need time to get to know new people. Perhaps a dear friend has moved away, and we are grieving the loss of that constant close-by friendship. Maybe a friend has hurt and rejected us, and we feel cast aside and abandoned. Whether we have close friends or are all alone, we can always trust in Jesus—our perfect friend.

He has known us and loved us since before time began. God chose us to be part of his family when we were still his enemies. He knows us better than any human friend ever will. He knitted us in our mother's womb and knew every part of us. He knows the thoughts and intentions of our hearts even before we know them ourselves. He created us for a purpose and with specific works in mind for us to do. He is our greatest friend.

Our Savior will never reject or abandon us. He will never grow tired of us and cast us aside. He went to great lengths to rescue us from sin. He laid down his own life for us. There is nothing we can do that will separate us from him. We can always rely on him. He is a faithful and steadfast friend.

At all times and in all places, he is with us. He hears the cries of our hearts. He knows our sins, our frailties, and our sorrows. He knows our deepest longings and our greatest needs. He always listens to us and responds to us. He meets us, right where we are, with love and grace. He is our forever friend.

When we feel lost and alone, when we have no one else to turn to, we can cry out to our Savior. We can share with him all our worries and fears, our hopes and dreams, our joys and sorrows. We can seek his wisdom in our mothering. We can receive his help in our troubles. He is always with us and will never leave us. What a friend we have in Jesus!

For a Mom's Heart

1. Read Romans 12:3–21. What do you learn about Christian community from this passage?
2. What does it mean to you that, because of Jesus, you are never alone?
3. Pray to the One who knows you inside and out. Seek his friendship at all times and in all places. Ask him to provide you with godly friendships in the body of Christ.

A Gospel Prayer for the Lonely

*No longer do I call you servants, for the servant does
not know what his master is doing; but I have called
you friends, for all that I have heard from my Father
I have made known to you. (John 15:15)*

Dear Father in heaven,

I come before you today feeling lonely. Isolated.
Unloved. I have had a hard day, and there is no one to
share it with. I have problems in my motherhood and
don't know who to ask for wisdom. I am so alone, and I
don't see any way out.

I thank you for Jesus, who calls me his friend. He
knows what it is like to be alone. He knows what it is like
to have friends turn on him and leave him. He knows
what it is like to not fit in with the crowd. He is a compassionate Savior. I thank you, Jesus, for being rejected
for my sake. You could have been loved by everyone. You
could have been crowned King. But you were despised
and rejected, treated as the worst of criminals—and
because you were, I am counted as your friend.

Forgive me for the times I reject others. Forgive me
when I expect people to be good friends to me and yet fail
to be a good friend to them. Forgive me for not participat-
ing in and being a part of the body of Christ. Forgive me
for not looking out for those who are friendless and not
inviting them into community. Forgive me for encouraging cliques and groups in the church, rather than seeking
to love and serve all the members of the body.

Help me to grow in my friendship with you and,

out of that friendship, to befriend others. When seasons of loneliness come, help me not to despair but to find solace in you. Help me to remember your perfect friendship with me. Even when I cannot trust others, and even when there is no one else to stand beside me, you are always with me.

Hear my heart's cry today. In Jesus's name, amen.

15

When Our Children
Are Hurting

In the Word we hear of God, but in affliction we see him.

Thomas Case

One of the hardest things about being a mom is watching our children struggle or suffer in some way.

When my oldest was four, he had to have sinus surgery. It was not only difficult to watch him go through it, but also difficult knowing that he didn't quite understand all that was happening. Even my attempts to explain that the pain he experienced was for a good reason—that it would ultimately make him better—was difficult.

It was heartbreaking to see my youngest grieve when his best friend moved far away. His life as he knew it had changed. He felt lost and lonely. All I could do was grieve with him.

For a year, one of my kids worked hard toward earning a belt in martial arts. He practiced the forms over and over. We helped to quiz him on the terms he had to memorize in Korean. When the time came to perform, he did not pass. It hurt to see him endure failure.

We live in a fallen world, and our children will endure heartache and suffering. It's one thing to acknowledge the truth of suffering in our own lives—it is harder to face it in our children's lives. If it were possible, we would bear their suffering for them. We love our children and don't want to see them go through hardships or trials.

Consider the painful circumstances your own child has endured. Learning struggles. Bullying. Loneliness. Loss and grief. Chronic health problems. Physical limitations. Traumatic experiences. Some mothers may not even know the full extent of the difficulties that their children experienced before being adopted into their forever family. And some, such as foster mothers, feel the weight of what has happened and of what may come when children leave the placement in their home. Each and every heartache is hard to watch. As moms, we want to jump in and protect our children. We want to take away their pain. We want to keep them from the hard things of life.

Certainly, we have a responsibility to keep our children from harm. We teach them to look both ways before they cross the street. We train them how to respond to suspicious people who offer them candy or ask them for help with finding a missing pet. We show them how to dial 911 in case of emergency and make them wear a helmet when they ride a bike. These are good and right things for us to do. There is wisdom in that.

But living in a fallen world means that we can't protect our children from everything. They may wear a helmet and still fall off their bike and break an arm. Accidents happen. We can't protect them from failure, either. No matter how much we invest in tutoring or training, they may still fail at something. They will also experience disappointment, heartache, and grief in their lives. They may not reach goals they pursue. They may even experience deep suffering. This is all hard to think about, but it's true.

The question is, what does the gospel have to say to this? How is Jesus our help and hope when our children suffer?

Why Jesus Came

We live in a broken world where things are not as they should be. In the prayer in chapter 4, I referred to the meta-story of Scripture. When we encounter suffering, it's important for us to remember the big story of the Bible because it explains to us why bad things happen. Because of the fall of Adam and Eve, sin permeated all creation. Bad things happen because of sin—because of sins that other people commit against us, because of sins that we commit and the resulting consequences of those sins, and because of the effects that sin has on the creation itself, including death, decay, and disease. Sometimes all these factors come into play at once.

This is why Jesus came. He came to redeem and restore the brokenness that sin causes. He came to make all things new. He came to set us free from sin and death. And he did so through his own suffering. "He himself bore our sins in his body on the tree, that we might die to sin and live to righteousness. By his wounds you have been healed" (1 Peter 2:24).

I often think about what Mary must have thought when Simeon said to her, at Jesus's circumcision,

Lord, now you are letting your servant depart in peace,
    according to your word;
for my eyes have seen your salvation
    that you have prepared in the presence of all peoples,
a light for revelation to the Gentiles,
    and for glory to your people Israel.

. . . Behold, this child is appointed for the fall and rising of many in Israel, and for a sign that is opposed (and a sword will pierce through your own soul also), so that thoughts from many hearts may be revealed. (Luke 2:29–32, 34–35)

She marveled and wondered at the good news of who Jesus was and how he would bring salvation. At the same time, how did she feel, knowing that grief lay ahead for her as well? What did it mean to her that her child would suffer one day? As Matthew Henry noted, "When he was abused, it was a sword in her bones. When she stood by his cross, and saw him dying, we may well think her inward grief was such that it might truly be said, a sword pierced through her soul, it cut her to the heart."[1]

That mixture of hope and heartache that Mary likely felt that day in the temple reflects the gospel. God used the worst atrocity—the suffering of Jesus Christ on the cross—to bring about the greatest good: our redemption from sin. By his wounds we were healed (see Isa. 53:5).

Suffering for Christ

The suffering and trials that we face in this life happen for a variety of reasons. As noted above, ultimately all suffering is rooted in sin and the fall of mankind. That's because hardships did not exist until after the fall. But, even so, we still may not know the specific reasons why we face a particular trial or season of suffering in this life. This was true of Job; he never knew why he endured the horrors that he did. We also can't assume that suffering is directly related to a person's own sin. When Jesus was asked by the disciples whether a man who had been born blind was blind because of his sin or his parent's sin, Jesus responded, "It was not that this man sinned, or his parents, but that the works of God might be displayed in him" (John 9:3).

For the believer, suffering is part of following Christ. "If anyone would come after me, let him deny himself and take up his

1. Matthew Henry, *Matthew Henry's Commentary on the Whole Bible* (Peabody, MA: Hendrickson Publishers, 1991), 1830.

cross and follow me" (Matt. 16:24). Just as our Savior suffered, we can expect to suffer in some way as well. He calls us to a life of suffering for his sake. In addition, God uses suffering for our sanctification—to train us and make us more like Christ.

In the case of our children, whether the Spirit has gripped their hearts yet or not, we can expect the Lord to use suffering in their lives for redemptive purposes. Consider the things you have experienced in your life that brought you to the cross of Christ. Perhaps it was a chronic health problem, or maybe a broken relationship. Maybe you experienced a significant loss in your life. It may be that you went through a season of rebellion and then experienced the consequences of that rebellion. Whatever your circumstances, the Lord used them to bring you to himself, to show you your need for him, to loosen your grip on this world.

Our children also need to see their need for Jesus. It may be through failures that they come to realize that they can't do life on their own. It may be through an illness or an accident that they come to depend on Christ. Maybe God will use your son's learning disability to help him to trust his Savior. It's possible that the loneliness your daughter is experiencing may be what God uses to help her reach out to and befriend someone who needs to know Christ. At some point in their lives, whether in childhood or adulthood, they will experience one or more hardships. The Lord may choose to use those hardships as a tool to show them their need for him and to bring them to himself.

As we moms see this happen, our hearts will ache and even break, but we have to remember that Jesus loves our children even more than we do. Our children were known by God before the creation of the world. They were created in God's image to live for him and his glory. Like all good gifts, our children were given to us so we could love and care for them—but ultimately, they belong to God. While we don't know exactly what God is doing when he allows hardships into our children's lives, we can be certain that he cares about our children's souls. He cares about who they are in eternity. Just as we trust the Lord's work in our own trials, we can trust the work he is doing in their lives.

This is something that we need to teach our own children as well. We need to model for them how to trust in God when they don't understand what is happening. When we experience our own trials, we can share these struggles with our children as a means of explaining that even though a trial is difficult, God is with us in it. We can point out to our children other people in their lives who have faced hardship and can explain how God met these people in their suffering with his sufficient grace. We can read to our children biographies of missionaries or of other laborers for the kingdom and can point out the hope and trust they displayed in God's sovereign care during their sufferings. Many of these stories show God's provision in amazing and remarkable ways.

Look to Christ

As we witness the hardships in our children's lives, it is important that we look to Christ and help our children to look to him as well.

We need to look to the gospel and remember who Christ is and what he did for us. We need to place our hope in his work of redemption, for he alone can save. Only he can redeem the trials and hardships that our children endure.

We must remember his preeminence over all things—including our children's hearts. When we worry or fear for our children because of the struggles they are going through, we must trust that the God who ordered the planets is the same God who orders the events in their lives. He is the author of their story; his name is on the cover. Only he knows the ending. When our hearts weep over the hard things our children face, we have to remember that our Savior weeps too. He grieves the sin and sorrow of this fallen world—so much so that he came to do something about it. He gave of his own life to seek and save the lost.

Our children need to hear the gospel as well. When they face difficulties and challenges in their lives, we need to teach them what happened in the fall and what God did to redeem them from sin. We need to point them to Jesus—to his perfect life, sacrificial death, triumphant resurrection, and ascension into heaven. If they have not already embraced the gospel by faith, we need to use their hardships as opportunities to share the gospel with them—to show them their need for Christ and what he has done. We can share with them our own testimonies of how the Lord brought us to faith in him. If our children have already proclaimed faith, we need to help them to see how their trials are opportunities for them to learn and grow in their faith, in their trust, and in their love for their Savior. We can share our own stories of God's work in and through suffering and can teach them how God uses suffering for our good and his glory.

As covenant children, our children are part of the community of faith. They receive many benefits from being a part of the church. They hear the gospel preached on Sunday mornings. They participate in corporate prayer, recite the gospel in the confessions, and sing praises to our Savior. Other church members mentor and disciple them in the faith. In all of this, our children learn the gospel. It becomes a part of the rhythm of their lives—and, we pray, the heartbeat of their soul.

My friend, we need to seek Jesus in our children's trials. We need to depend on him and his grace to see our children through their struggles. We need to hope in the gospel and in the power of the Spirit to work in our children's hearts. May all their struggles bring them (and us) to the feet of Jesus.

For a Mom's Heart

1. Read 1 Peter 1. What is our (and our children's) hope when trials come?
2. How does the gospel give you hope in the midst of your children's hardships?
3. Turn to God in prayer. Pray for his work in your children's lives—that the hardships they endure would be used for their eternal good.

A Gospel Prayer for When Our Children Are Hurting

For to this you have been called, because Christ also suffered for you, leaving you an example, so that you might follow in his steps. He committed no sin, neither was deceit found in his mouth. When he was reviled, he did not revile in return; when he suffered, he did not threaten, but continued entrusting himself to him who judges justly. (1 Peter 2:21–23)

Dear Father,

I come before you with a broken heart. I weep over my child's suffering and pain. I want to cry out, "Why, Lord? Why my child?" I want to take away the pain. I wish I could make it mine instead.

But then I remember that you understand what it's like to see your own Son suffer. Before time began, you planned a way to rescue us from sin—by having your own Son suffer for us. You saw him tortured, beaten, and bruised. You heard him weep in the garden as he considered the weight of his suffering to come. And then you laid out your wrath on him, which we deserved.

Forgive me when I forget the hope that I have in the gospel. Forgive me when I don't look at my children's sufferings through the lens of what Jesus did, but instead look for someone or something to blame. Or attempt to wrap my children up in protective bubble wrap, in the hopes that nothing bad will happen to them. Or live in despair.

Father, please redeem this hardship in my child's life. If it be your will, remove it. If it is not your will to remove it, please use it for your glory and their good. Use it to draw them to yourself and the gospel. Use it to change and sanctify them. Use it to shape their hearts for eternity. And use it in my own heart to draw me nearer to you.

Suffering loosens my grip on this world and makes me long for my eternal home. Please come quickly, Lord! Come and make your home with us. Give us new bodies and new hearts. I long to sing your praises before the throne of God.

Until that day comes, help me and my children to live for you, even in the hardships and trials of life.

In Jesus's name, amen.

16

Mommy Guilt

We have dreadfully provoked God, but Christ has performed
that righteousness which is infinitely precious in God's eyes.

JONATHAN EDWARDS

My youngest son was diagnosed with asthma at six weeks old. When he was in preschool, constant sickness exacerbated his condition. We were vigilant with his breathing treatments. I did all I could to prevent him from being sick, but, short of placing him in a protective bubble, I couldn't keep him from catching one thing after another. The doctors ran tests and tried different medications. One medication that they tried was specifically for asthma prevention.

A month or so went by, and my son grew more and more irritable. Sad. Almost depressed. We talked with him and prayed with him. We tried to figure out what was bothering him. He cried about everything. It hurt us to see him so sad, but we couldn't determine what was bothering him. He didn't even know.

And then I remembered the new medication. I did some research and learned that depression was a potential side effect. I immediately called the doctor and discontinued it.

I still remember the mommy guilt I felt. My son was hurting, and I didn't know how to help him. When I realized that a medication was to blame, I felt guilty that I hadn't read the side effects before I gave it to him. I felt guilty that it had taken me so long to figure out the source of his sadness. I felt guilty that he had suffered.

That's not the only time I have felt that way. I've often felt that I've let my children down by not being the mom they needed me to be. I've felt angry at myself for missing things I should have caught. I've bemoaned the weaknesses and insufficiencies that have kept me from providing for or meeting my children's needs at all times and in all places.

Mommy guilt. At some point in our motherhood, we will experience it. Our child may have an illness we were slow to detect. Our son might have a learning problem for years before we realize it. Our daughter might complain about other kids picking on her, which we disregard until she comes home in tears, afraid to go to school. Whatever the circumstances, we know that feeling of guilt when our children are hurt. We feel responsible. It weighs heavily on our hearts. We can't stop thinking of how bad the situation could have been. We consider all the additional ways it could have been worse. We vow to be more vigilant in the future.

If motherhood were a job, we'd likely have fired ourselves by now.

True Guilt vs. False Guilt

As moms, we tend to hold ourselves to a high standard. We demand and expect more of ourselves than we would of anyone else. We try to be all things to all people. We expect ourselves to know everything, be everything, and be capable of everything.

When it comes to our kids, we expect ourselves to know that they are sick before anyone else does. We expect ourselves to never forget to take them to an appointment or overlook atypical behavior. We expect to always be on top of things and to never miss that they've been secretive or that their best friend stopped hanging around or that their appetite is off. We expect ourselves to know immediately if they are behind their peers academically or are having trouble fitting in with other kids on the playground.

And when we do miss something, we berate ourselves. We've let our children down—and as a result, we deserve the Worst Mom of the Year award. But the truth is that the guilt we feel isn't true guilt. True guilt is the result of sin. When we sin and break God's law, we are guilty. In fact, we are all guilty; because, as James reminds us, "Whoever keeps the whole law but fails in one point has become guilty of all of it" (James 2:10).

However, missing something is not sin. Forgetting something or failing to prevent something is not sin. Being ignorant or lacking knowledge about something is human frailty, not sin. When our child gets hurt and we can't stop it from happening, that is a human limitation, not sin. When something happens that we don't know about, that's because our knowledge is limited to a specific time and place. That too is not sin; it's a reflection of our humanity.

We are finite human beings—we are not God. We cannot know or foresee the future for our children. We cannot know everything about our children. We cannot control everything that happens. We cannot prevent things from happening. We are limited by our humanity. We make mistakes. We miss things. We forget things.

It's important that when we feel the weight of guilt on our hearts, we determine whether what we're feeling is true guilt or false guilt. Have we sinned, and do we need to come to God and repent of that sin? Or are we simply human?

Acknowledging our human frailty and limitations is hard for us as moms. We try to be the best mom for our children—which is a noble task and aspiration. But the reality is that, try as we might, we cannot control everything. We cannot know everything. Things will happen that we did not expect or anticipate. Our human weaknesses and limitations will interfere in some way. And that's when we have to face the truth: we are not perfect.

You know what? All but one of the people whom God used in his plan of redemption were not perfect either. They had weaknesses and limitations too. By the world's standards, they had nothing to offer. Take Moses, for example. He had a stutter and was an unlikely candidate for leadership. But God used him to lead the Israelites out of slavery. David was a young shepherd boy, the youngest of his family, yet God chose him to be king. Mary was young, poor, and insignificant, yet God used her to be the mother of our Savior. The apostle Peter was an uneducated fisherman who often spoke without thinking first, yet God made him the "rock" and an important leader in the early church.

Yes, we are imperfect as moms. Yes, we fail our children from time to time. But God has called us to this important task, and he will make us who we need to be for our children. How will he do that? Through Christ.

Our Perfect Savior

Our Savior is the second person of the Trinity. He is God incarnate. He is "the radiance of the glory of God and the exact imprint of his nature, and he upholds the universe by the word of his power. After making purification for sins, he sat down at the right hand of the Majesty on high" (Heb. 1:3). Our Savior rules and governs all things. He is sovereign over all things. He knows all things. He is always fully present, and he never overlooks or misses anything. He is perfect, holy, and righteous. That's why he was our substitute at the cross. He was the Lamb without blemish—the only one who could take on our sins.

He also knows all of his creation, from the least to the greatest—including the small sparrow (see Luke 12:6). He cares for and about his creation, from protecting the cattle on the hill (see Jonah 4:11) to providing rain for the barren desert (see Job 38:26) to feeding the hungry raven (Job 38:41). If he cares for his creation, how much more does he care for us, whom he made in his image? Our Lord knows all our cares and meets all our needs. He is loving, kind, and compassionate. "For the LORD is good; his steadfast love endures forever, and his faithfulness to all generations" (Ps. 100:5). He always does what is consistent with his character.

God has proven his faithfulness time and time again. His ultimate act of faithfulness was securing our redemption from sin at the cross. If he was faithful to save us from our sins, we can be certain that he will be faithful to us in our motherhood.

When we feel guilty because of our failure to meet our children's needs, we need to turn to Jesus. When we are imperfect and weak, we need to rest in him. When we face the reality that we cannot control all things, we need to trust in him. We need to remember who he is. Jesus Christ is everything that we cannot be. He is our Redeemer who obeyed the law that we couldn't obey, resisted the temptations that we couldn't resist, and trusted God when we failed to. He is our strength in our weakness, our sufficiency in our insufficiency, our wisdom in our ignorance. Jesus Christ is perfect for us.

An Example from Paul

In a letter to the Corinthian church, Paul described his ministry to them.

And I, when I came to you, brothers, did not come proclaiming to you the testimony of God with lofty speech or wisdom. For

I decided to know nothing among you except Jesus Christ and him crucified. And I was with you in weakness and in fear and much trembling, and my speech and my message were not in plausible words of wisdom, but in demonstration of the Spirit and of power, so that your faith might not rest in the wisdom of men but in the power of God. (1 Cor. 2:1–5)

One of the problems plaguing the Corinthian church was the confidence they had placed in human wisdom and strength. That is why Paul did not preach to them using Grecian arguments or fancy speeches. He spoke with weakness and human frailty so that the Spirit and the power of the gospel would be exalted. He wanted them to know Christ. He wanted them to notice not him, and what he could do, but what God could do through him.

Paul's goal and our goal as moms are the same: to know nothing except Jesus Christ and him crucified. We don't trust in human wisdom or strength. We don't rely on ourselves and our abilities. We don't place confidence in who we are and what we can do; we place it in who Christ is and in the power of the gospel at work in us.

My friend, if you struggle with mommy guilt, remember who you are as a weak and finite creature. Also remember who your God is. You are not perfect, but Christ is. Find your hope in the gospel and in who Christ is for you.

For a Mom's Heart

1. Read 1 Corinthians 1:26–31. Why does God choose the weak? Who do we boast in?
2. Are you ever angry with yourself for failing to be the perfect mom? What does the gospel have to say to you?
3. Turn to God in prayer. Admit your weaknesses and limitations as a mom. Ask God to be your wisdom and strength.

A Gospel Prayer for the
Mom Who Feels Guilty

*For the foolishness of God is wiser than men, and the
weakness of God is stronger than men. (1 Cor. 1:25)*

Dear Father in heaven,
 I did it again. I failed as a mom. I let my children
down, and now they are hurting as a result. I feel like a
lousy mom. I should be fired. I'm not fit to be a mom.
I am weak and insufficient. I simply don't know enough.
 My response to this situation points to my perfec-
tionism and my desire to get everything right. I want to
be the best mom. I don't ever want to fail. Forgive me,
Father, for trying to do and be something that I cannot
be. Forgive me for relying on my own strength. Forgive
me for not trusting in you.
 You alone are God. You alone are perfect and righteous. You alone are sovereign over all things. You know
the end from the beginning and hold the world in the
palm of your hands. You know every detail of my life, my
failures as a mom, and all my children's needs.
 I thank you for your Son, Jesus, who is perfect for
me. He lived a perfect life and provided the perfect sacrifice for my sins. Because he was perfect, the grave did
not hold him. He rose to life and now reigns in heaven.
Because of who he is and what he has done, I don't have
to be a superhero mom. I can rest in who Jesus is for me.
 Be my strength this day. Be my wisdom. Be my hope.
In Jesus's name, amen.

17

The Gospel for Good Days

God is more rich, and more ready to give to his children
than the fathers of our flesh can be; for he is the Father
of our spirits, an ever-loving, ever-living Father.

MATTHEW HENRY

"Mom, this is the best trip ever!" my youngest exclaimed.

We had traveled to visit family in Anchorage and, as a special treat, taken the kids on a dog-sledding ride on top of a glacier. Other than the two dog trainers who lived on the ice field, we were the only people there.

We arrived by helicopter, flying over rocky mountain crags and seemingly endless miles of snow and ice. Everything was blindingly white as the sun shone down on the snow. The trainers taught us about the sled dogs and how they were trained, then took us on a sled ride with them. We laughed and shouted and loved every moment of it.

I had to agree with my son: it was the best trip. Not so much because we had a new experience, however—as thrilling as that was—but because we had that experience together. We made great memories as a family during that trip—ones we still talk about together.

Most of the chapters in this book have looked at how the gospel applies to the struggles and challenges we face as moms. This chapter looks at what the gospel has to say to our good days. Because there are many good days in motherhood.

Days such as

- when you meet your child for the first time, whether through birth or through adoption
- when your child accomplishes something for the very first time, such as taking her first steps, learning to ride a bike, reading her first words in a book, or performing in her first play
- when you laugh together over a silly joke
- when your son sits on your lap and snuggles while you read to him before bed
- when your daughter unwraps a present that you bought her, and her face lights up with joy
- when you watch your child accomplish something for which he's worked so hard
- when you enjoy a trip together and see God's creation on magnificent display
- when your child makes a public profession of faith
- when you witness the fruit of the Spirit at work in your child's heart

Such good days are a gift from the Lord. But sometimes we get so involved in the moment that we overlook what God shows us and shares with us in those good days. God has something for us in the good days of motherhood. Something that we don't want to miss.

Good Days Point Us to the Gospel

Our good days point us to who God is and what he has done for us in Christ.

God is the creator and giver of all good things. He gives us our very life, breath, and health (see Acts 17:25). He sustains us each day. He provides our needs. He puts lonely people in families. He gave us the gift of salvation, the Holy Spirit, and the promise of eternity. He uses our gifts and abilities for the good of the church. Indeed, all that we have, all that we are, comes to us by the hand of God. This includes our good days and sweet moments with our children.

God gives us good things because he is our Father. Through our salvation, we are adopted into God's family and become his children. And he is a *good* Father. He loves to shower his grace upon his children. He loves to give us good things to enjoy. From the food that we eat to the roofs over our heads, from fellowship with dear friends to the love of our families—all are good and generous gifts from God. Consider all the effort we put into providing good things for our children—how much more does our perfect heavenly Father give us exactly what we need when we need it! As Jesus said, "If you then, who are evil, know how to give good gifts to your children, how much more will your Father who is in heaven give good things to those who ask him!" (Matt. 7:11).

Our good days remind us that all things come to us from our good and gracious Father in heaven. They point us to who he is—to his goodness and kindness. In fact, we could think of those good days as a way in which God communicates to us something about himself. We can look at the fun moments with our children as a snapshot of God's goodness—of his love and faithfulness to us.

Consider the joy we feel over catching a sunset. It's more than a beautiful dance of color and light; it's the glory and wonder of God on display. Upon seeing that sunset, we marvel and rejoice at our creator God who made the processes that work together to produce a sunset: the rays of light that strike molecules in the atmosphere, which then shoot waves of light in different directions, producing hues of orange and red, pink and purple. We enjoy God as we enjoy his creation. We can't help but join with creation and sing his praises (see Ps. 19). When we enjoy the gift of God's creation, we are drawn into his wonder and magnificence, and we learn more about who our God is. He speaks to us about who he is in the gifts that he gives us.

What might God be communicating in that precious moment when we are sitting with our son or daughter and reading their favorite story as they snuggle up close on the couch? What can we learn about our God? How can we enjoy and marvel at who he is in that moment? For one, the love and affection that we feel for our children helps us to appreciate, all the greater, the fatherly love that God has for us. As much as we love our children, how much more does God love us! In fact, Jesus said that the Father loves us as much as he loves the Son (see John 17:23). Take a moment to consider that—isn't that amazing? Our love for our children, as strong as it is, pales in comparison to the perfect love that God has for us. His love for us began in eternity past; he loved us before time began. He loved us before we ever gave a thought to him. Even now, when our love for him is imperfect and at times wavers, his love for us never fails. He is always patient, kind, and forgiving.

In that sweet moment with our child, we can also marvel at the depths of God's sacrifice for us in Christ as we consider the ways that we sacrifice for our own children. What we wouldn't do for our children! Consider all the sacrifices you've made for your children: sacrifices of time, money, energy, and more. The sacrifices that we make each day remind us of the greater sacrifice that God made for us. Good days remind us of the gospel—that God so loved us that he sent his only Son to save us from our sins.

As we appreciate and enjoy those good days—which he wants us to do!—we also need to remember that we don't deserve any of God's good gifts to us. In fact, the gospel tells us that because of sin, we deserve death (Rom. 6:23). But God, in his grace, loved us in Christ. "God shows his love for us in that while we were still sinners, Christ died for us" (Rom. 5:8). That is the greatest gift of all! All good gifts point to the ultimate gift: salvation in Christ. They point us to our Savior and remind us of all the blessings that we have because of what Christ has done for us in his life, death, resurrection, and ascension.

While good days point us to who God is and what he has done for us, they also point us to the better and glorious days to come. Because Christ has secured salvation for us and a home forever with him in eternity, good days remind us of the perfect days that lie ahead. One day, sin and sorrow will be no more, and only joy will remain. The brief moments of joy that we experience here are just a shadow—a foretaste of the everlasting joy we will experience when we see Christ face-to-face.

Give Thanks for Good Days

What do we tell our children when someone gives them a gift? We tell them to say, "Thank you." That's because saying thank you is the appropriate response to receiving a gift. How much more should we respond in thanksgiving to our great God for all he has done for us!

Those good days of motherhood are wonderful opportunities for us to enjoy our children. They are also opportunities for us to enjoy and marvel at and praise our great God. Good days open our eyes so we can see and trace God's grace in our lives in fresh ways. They invite us to worship him.

When we take time to see God in our good days with our children, we ought to respond in thanksgiving for who he is. We thank him that he is the Maker and Sustainer of all things. We thank him for his awesome power and might. We thank him for his character, holiness, goodness, and faithfulness. We thank him for his great and steadfast love for us. As the psalmist wrote, "Great is the LORD and most worthy of praise; his greatness no one can fathom" (Ps. 145:3 NIV) and "Oh give thanks to the LORD, for he is good, for his steadfast love endures forever!" (Ps. 107:1).

Good days also remind us to give thanks for all that God has done for us. When we see his goodness to us in special trips with our families, we ought to give thanks. When we see his faithfulness in our children's growth in faith, we ought to rejoice in what he has done. When we see his love for us in Christ in our own love for our children, we ought to respond with thanksgiving. "Therefore let us be grateful for receiving a kingdom that cannot be shaken, and thus let us offer to God acceptable worship, with reverence and awe" (Heb. 12:28).

The good days that God gives us are a gift—a precious gift that is not to be overlooked. As with all gifts we receive, we ought to respond with thanksgiving and praise.

So let us cherish and treasure every good day that God gives us. May those days not only point us to who God is and what he has done but also draw us to worship and praise our great God. May we see God in those days and pause in those moments to thank the Lord for his goodness and love to us. May we praise him for who he is and for all he has done for us in Christ.

For a Mom's Heart

1. Read Psalm 136. What kinds of things does the psalmist sing praises to God for?
2. The passage above looked at God's faithfulness to Israel.

Write your own praises to God. Write down what God has done in your life (including giving you the gift of salvation) and add, after each line, "for his steadfast love endures forever."

3. Pray the prayer of praise you've just written.

A Gospel Prayer of Thanks in Good Days

Oh, taste and see that the LORD is good! (Ps. 34:8)

Father in heaven,

What a joy and privilege it is to call you my Father! I thank you that you are a good Father. I thank you for all the good gifts that you give me—gifts I do not deserve, but gifts that you give me out of your great love for me in Christ.

I thank you for the sweet day we've had together as a family. I thank you for the growth and maturity I've seen in my children. I thank you for the opportunities you provide for us to enjoy your creation together.

Forgive me for the ways I have not seen you in the good gifts that you give us. Forgive me for the ways my heart worships the good days of motherhood and seeks to find my hope in them. Forgive me for failing to give you the praise and honor you are due for all the gifts that you give us.

Help me to see you in the gifts that you give—to see your hand at work in the good days of motherhood. Help me to learn more about who you are in those moments. Help me to remember the good news of the gospel in those days. May those days remind me of the joy that is mine forever in eternity, when I will live and worship you forever.

In Jesus's name, amen.

Conclusion

As a mom, I've spent countless hours of my life reading books to my children. If there were a category in the *Guinness Book of World Records* for the number of times *Goodnight Moon* has been read, I would certainly win. Usually, when we would get to the end of a story, I'd say, "The end." And we'd move on to the next book. (Though in truth, my children often responded with, "Again! Read it again!")

That's often what we do as adults—we read a book, put it back on the shelf, and start another one. While you might place this book back on your bookshelf, and though you may not read it over and over as we do with our children's books, my prayer is that the truths of the gospel it points to will not be something that you leave behind. You need the gospel every day of your life.

In every moment—joyous or painful, exciting or mundane, easy or difficult—the gospel provides moms with real and lasting hope. The truths of who Jesus is and what he came to do through his life, death, resurrection, and ascension don't just impact us at the moment of our salvation; they intersect with our daily lives and bring life-giving hope.

When I use the word *hope*, I don't mean it in the way many

people do. People often use the word *hope* to indicate a wish. "I hope you feel better." "I hope it doesn't rain tomorrow." "I hope we get home on time." Such hope has no power. It's like sending someone happy thoughts—as though our thoughts alone could do anything to heal a person or hold back the rain or make the roads free from traffic. Often, such hopes let us down. We hope for a better day today than the one we had yesterday, only to find that we are living out the '90s classic *Groundhog Day*. Wash. Rinse. Repeat.

The Bible, however, uses the word *hope* in a more certain and concrete way. Not as a wish but as a real thing. Hope is tangible—something we can grasp. It is a foregone conclusion. "We have this as a sure and steadfast anchor of the soul, a hope that enters into the inner place behind the curtain" (Heb. 6:19).

Such hope is a confident expectation of God's future grace in our lives, which is grounded in his past grace. We can look forward with hope because of what God has done for us in Christ. Ultimately, hope is a person: Christ, our living hope.

> Blessed be the God and Father of our Lord Jesus Christ! According to his great mercy, he has caused us to be born again to a *living hope* through the resurrection of Jesus Christ from the dead, to an inheritance that is imperishable, undefiled, and unfading, kept in heaven for you, who by God's power are being guarded through faith for a salvation ready to be revealed in the last time. (1 Peter 1:3–5)

That's why we look to the gospel, study it, appropriate it, and remember it. As you close this book, I want to leave you with a few questions to ask yourself as you go about your day and mother the eternal souls God has placed in your care. These questions remind you of your hope—of who Christ is and what he has done.

- In this challenging moment, what does the gospel have to say to me? How does what Jesus did for me provide hope in this trial I am in right now?
- In my weakness and helplessness, how does the perfect life Jesus lived for me meet me where I am and provide real hope?
- In my sinful responses to my child today, how does Jesus's sacrificial death cover my sin?
- What does Jesus's resurrection and his promise to make all things new say to my child's battle with sin today?
- How does Jesus's ascension into heaven, where he sits at the right hand of God, meet me in this day when everything seems to be going wrong and the chaos is overwhelming?

As you consider such questions, stop and take a moment to pray through the gospel and apply those truths to what is happening in your life. Tell the Lord about your worries and fears. Tell him that you feel helpless, or insufficient, or weary and worn. Confess your sinful thoughts, attitudes, and responses. Pray through the truths of the gospel and appropriate them to your life and heart.

Remembering the gospel and preaching it to ourselves isn't something that we do on occasion; it's a daily habit. A holy habit—one that becomes part of the rhythm and heartbeat of our lives. This is not a habit that is done without meaning. It's not a rote habit that we do without even thinking about what we're doing, like brushing our teeth or driving to work. It's a life-sustaining habit—one that breathes life into our circumstances and anchors us during trials and storms. It's a habit that helps us to abide in Christ—to draw from his abundant supply of grace. And ultimately it's a habit that points us to our Savior—our living hope.

Dear friend, may Jesus be your hope—now and always.

Christina Fox

Gospel-Centered Resources for Moms

I wanted to provide a few resources that will aid you with reciting the gospel in your daily life. These gospel-centered resources point to the truths of who Jesus is and what he came to do, and they will help you apply those truths to various aspects of your life.

For Your Heart

Bridges, Jerry. *The Discipline of Grace: God's Role and Our Role in the Pursuit of Holiness.* 1994. Reprint, Colorado Springs: NavPress, 2006.

Duguid, Barbara R. *Extravagant Grace: God's Glory Displayed in Our Weakness.* Phillipsburg, NJ: P&R Publishing, 2013.

Fitzpatrick, Elyse M. *Because He Loves Me: How Christ Transforms Our Daily Life.* 2008. Reprint, Wheaton, IL: Crossway, 2010.

———. *Comforts from the Cross: Celebrating the Gospel One Day at a Time.* 2009. Reprint, Wheaton, IL: Crossway, 2011.

Hill, Megan. *Contentment: Seeing God's Goodness.* Phillipsburg, NJ: P&R Publishing, 2018.

Horton, Michael. *The Gospel-Driven Life: Being Good News People in a Bad News World.* 2009. Reprint, Grand Rapids: Baker Books, 2012.

Keller, Timothy. *The Freedom of Self-Forgetfulness: The Path to True Christian Joy*. Youngstown, OH: 10Publishing, 2012.

Smith, Scotty. *Everyday Prayers: 365 Days to a Gospel-Centered Faith*. Grand Rapids: Baker Books, 2011.

———. *Every Season Prayers: Gospel-Centered Prayers for the Whole of Life*. Grand Rapids: Baker Books, 2016.

Tripp, Paul David. *New Morning Mercies: A Daily Gospel Devotional*. Wheaton, IL: Crossway, 2014.

For Your Motherhood

Fitzpatrick, Elyse, and Jessica Thompson. *Answering Your Kids' Toughest Questions: Helping Them Understand Loss, Sin, Tragedies, and Other Hard Topics*. Bloomington, MN: Bethany House, 2014.

———. *Give Them Grace: Dazzling Your Kids with the Love of Jesus*. Wheaton, IL: Crossway, 2011.

Furman, Gloria. *Treasuring Christ When Your Hands Are Full: Gospel Meditations for Busy Moms*. Wheaton, IL: Crossway, 2014.

Kruger, Melissa B. *Walking with God in the Season of Motherhood: An Eleven-Week Devotional Bible Study*. Colorado Springs: Waterbrook, 2015.

Mackle, Holly, and Linda Barrett. *Engaging Motherhood: Heart Preparation for a Holy Calling*. Lawrenceville, GA: PCA CDM, 2016.

Miller, Rose Marie, Deborah Harrell, and Jack Klumpenhower. *The Gospel-Centered Parent: Study Guide with Leader's Notes*. Greensboro, NC: New Growth, 2015.

Reissig, Courtney. *Glory in the Ordinary: Why Your Work in the Home Matters to God*. Wheaton, IL: Crossway, 2017.

Thompson, Jessica, and Joel Fitzpatrick. *Mom, Dad . . . What's Sex?: Giving Your Kids a Gospel-Centered View of Sex and Our Culture*. Eugene, OR: Harvest House, 2018.

Tripp, Paul David. *Age of Opportunity: A Biblical Guide to Parenting Teens*. Phillipsburg, NJ: P&R Publishing, 2001.